Measuring Customer Service Effectiveness

Measuring Customer Service Effectiveness

SARAH COOK

GOWER

Published by
Gower Publishing Limited
Gower House
Croft Road
Aldershot
Hants GU11 3HR
England

Gower Publishing Company
Suite 420
101 Cherry Street
Burlington,
VT 05401-4405
USA

Sarah Cook has asserted her right under the Copyright, Designs and Patents Act 1988 to be identified as the author of this work.

British Library Cataloguing in Publication Data
A catalogue record for this book is available from the British Library.

Library of Congress Cataloging-in-Publication Data
Cook, Sarah, 1955–
  Measuring customer service effectiveness / by Sarah Cook.
    p. cm.
  Includes bibliographical references and index.
  ISBN: 0-566-08538-0
 1. Customer services--Quality control. 2. Customer services--Evaluation. 3. Customer services--Management . I. Title.
  HF5415.5.C6636 2004
   658.8'12--dc22

                                                                                              2004007805

Typeset in 9 point Stone Serif by IML Typographers, Birkenhead, Merseyside and printed in Great Britain by MPG Books Ltd, Bodmin, Cornwall.

Contents

List of Figures

Introduction

Welcome to *Measuring Customer Service Effectiveness*. This book is designed as a practical guide to measuring both external and internal service quality in your organisation. Whether you are a senior manager responsible for service excellence, line manager, team leader, human resources (HR), learning and development professional or management consultant, measuring the effectiveness of the service you and your organisation provides is critical to business success.

The contents of the book follow a logical sequence:

- 'Why measure' is contained in Chapter 1.
- Hints and tips on 'Preparing to measure' are contained in Chapter 2.
- In Chapters 3 and 4 I discuss methods of gaining quantitative as well as qualitative research data from customers.
- The quality of internal customer service is a key determinant of the quality of external customer service. I discuss how to measure internal service in Chapter 5.
- Chapter 6 focuses on benchmarking and benchmarking techniques.
- Analysing and effectively communicating the results of customer service measurement is addressed in Chapter 7.
- In Chapter 8 I make suggestions on what actions you can take as a result of measuring customer service.

Each chapter begins with an overview of the content of the chapter. It ends with a checklist to help you assess what actions you need to take to put the learning from the chapter into practice.

As part of the agenda for public service reform and delivery, over the last few years far greater emphasis has been placed on measurement of performance in the public sector than in earlier years. In particular, the spotlight has fallen on customer satisfaction. All of the customer service measurement techniques in this book are applicable to both the private and the public sector. They are drawn from our experience of working across a wide range of industry sectors.

I hope that you find the book a useful reference guide.

Sarah Cook
Stairway Consultancy

Acknowledgements

Much of the content of this book is based on the practical experience I have gained at The Stairway Consultancy in helping organisations in the public and private sectors to measure and improve their customer service. Thanks go also to Sylvia Ainley, Client Support Manager at Stairway, who provided valuable assistance in the research phase of this book.

1 *The Business Case for Measurement*

Return on investment in customer service

A study undertaken by the Institute of Customer Service in 2001 found that those organisations with an excellent reputation in their customers' eyes demonstrated a 72 per cent increase in profit per employee on a like for like basis compared with those companies with a poor reputation. They also produced a higher net margin and a higher return on total assets. Their employees were more highly motivated and shared well articulated values and good leadership. The latter demonstrated itself in openness, being in touch with the customer, a no-blame culture, trust, passion and lack of complacency.

There is ample research that demonstrates that outstanding service leads to enhanced profits and growth. Allan Leighton, chairman of the Royal Mail, says: 'The test of legendary customer service is: do your sales go up? Sales are the biggest measure of customer service,' (Customer Management Conference, May 2003).

So how do you measure customer service and its impact on the organisation? In this chapter we discuss:

- why customer service measurement is a key component of a service strategy;
- the service-value chain and the need for internal as well as external measures;
- using measurement to encourage innovation and continuous improvement.

WHAT GETS MEASURED, GETS DONE

An old adage but true. In many service organisations however, customer measurement can be an infrequent and haphazard event, the results of which are not properly communicated or acted upon.

Research proves that on average it costs five times as much to attract a new customer as it does to keep an existing one. Service measurement therefore plays a vital role in helping to:

- listen to customers
- establish what is important in their eyes
- assess your current performance against their expectations
- establish the lifetime value of customers
- understand why customers defect
- set the agenda for where your service provision needs to be as opposed to where it is now
- review and monitor progress of service improvement initiatives
- encourage innovation
- foster a climate of continuous improvement
- encourage customer loyalty, retention and, ultimately, profit.

Listening to the customer

- What is important?
- What do customers need?
- How does the service they receive now match their needs?
- What will make customers become advocates of the organisation?

Set and act on improvement agenda

- Communicate need for change
- Enhance existing service
- Develop new services

Figure 1.1   The process of customer service measurement

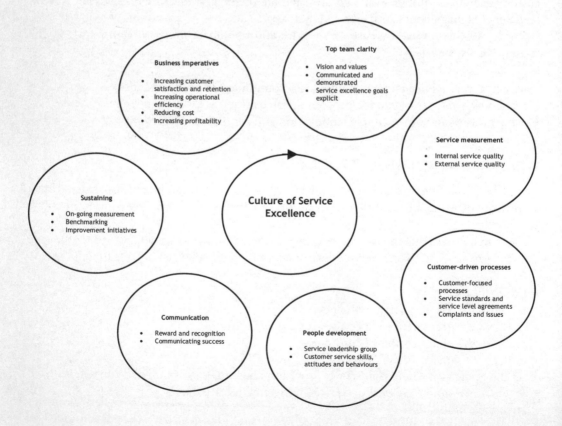

Figure 1.2   Measurement and service strategy

Customer service measurement should be an on-going and incremental process of assessment, planning for improvement, implementing improvement and review, as shown in Figure 1.1.

Measurement and service strategy

Best practice organisations have a service strategy encompassing all of their business that directs and guides their approach to service excellence. So where should service measurement sit in relation to service strategy? Figure 1.2 illustrates a typical strategy that incorporates service measurement.

My experience of working with a wide number of public and private sector organisations shows that measurement is a key element in an organisation's service strategy. It is the linchpin without which a service strategy cannot be built, since customer feedback provides evidence that will ensure the service strategy is driven by customers. For example, one client organisation with whom I worked found that, having recently installed an automated voice mail system, the response from customers was extremely poor. Customers were looking for a personal yet accessible service. Research conducted at the same time amongst employees showed poor levels of employee satisfaction, lack of trust and respect. Senior managers shared the outputs of these two studies with their teams. Subsequently a service strategy was designed to take both internal and external customer needs into account. The output was a more personalised service delivered to external customers, brought about as a result of breaking down internal barriers.

PUTTING THE CUSTOMER AT THE HEART OF THE BUSINESS

Measuring customer service is like telephoning one's parents. We all know we should do it and indeed it's a good thing to do, but some people phone every day, others each week and some leave it months or years. Likewise, best practice service organisations make customer service a core business competency, while other organisations do not value it or put customer measurement on their organisational radar.

Retail organisations such as Tesco have taken great strides in recent years to become more customer focused. They realised from the start that the change process would be lengthy – on average, culture change takes between three to five years. Making customer service a key business imperative was critical to their successful implementation of the change.

A critical determinant of making a business customer focused is whether leaders throughout the business not only talk about customer service being a key strategic aim, but furthermore, whether they talk the talk. People need to see consistency between what leaders say and do. For example, at food chain store Pret A Manger, all head office staff and managers spend a day a month working in stores to keep in touch with customers. They arrive when the store opens at 6.30 a.m. to make sandwiches and serve customers for the day. In this way support staff and management keep in touch with both customers and front-line employees.

To be successful, an organisation's vision, strategy, values and behaviour (see Figure 1.3) need to be aligned to the customer. Not only do senior managers need to be credible in how they communicate the importance of the customer to their employees, but they must also show through their actions that they believe this.

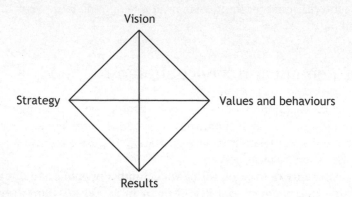

Figure 1.3   Vision, strategy, values, results

So how does *lack* of credible commitment to a service strategy affect service measurement?

A study by research organisation Customer Champions shows that 65 per cent of the results of customer feedback are not listened to or acted upon. Why is this? My conclusion is that as many senior managers do not believe that listening to customers is a key business imperative; they do not put effort into acting on the results of customer feedback. Furthermore they do not measure whether any action has been taken as a result of the feedback.

Typically organisations undertaking customer research have not thought through how they will subsequently use the findings or whose support they need to elicit to make the necessary changes. The research in itself is not linked to key business imperatives. Before undertaking any form of measurement, therefore, ask yourself:

- Do I have a sponsor for the research at the highest level of the organisation?
- Do I have the support of my immediate manager for the research?
- Do I know how I will use the findings?
- Do I have a strategy for communicating the findings?
- Do I know who will be instrumental in bringing about possible changes?
- How will I elicit their buy-in and support for the changes?

In Chapter 2 I discuss further the process for gaining support for the findings of customer service feedback.

What to measure

A further reason why customer research is not acted upon is because people do not measure the right things. Customer service is an intangible thing (it is an experience), it is perishable (the same experience happens only once) and it is personal (the experience is individual to the customer). As such it involves customers' *perception* of the *experience*.

Typically customer surveys are written by the service providers, setting out what the service providers want to know and on their own terms. For example measuring customers' opinions of:

- the product or service they received
- the price they paid, or value for money
- how the product or service was promoted
- the distribution channel.

Often customer measurement neglects to ask: 'What was the experience like of dealing with us? How did it feel to deal with us? What is important to the customer?'

It is the customer's perception that is the most important – perception is reality. Customer research should be driven from the customer's viewpoint, asking questions that the customer deems are important and in a way that is most helpful. In later chapters I provide examples of how you can do this.

MEASURE INTERNAL SERVICE QUALITY AS WELL AS EXTERNAL SERVICE QUALITY

Research by Heskett, Sasser and Schlesinger of the Harvard Business School demonstrated a clear link between what happens inside the organisation and the quality of the service provided to the external customer. In their book *The service profit chain* (The Free Press, New

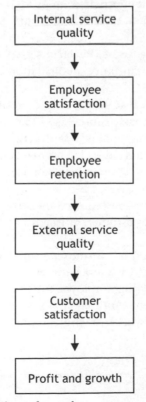

Figure 1.4   External and internal service and growth

York, 1997), the three Harvard professors show how leading service organisations grow and develop profitable businesses. They demonstrated a quantifiable set of relationships that link profit and growth not only to customer loyalty and satisfaction derived from good external service quality (how customers perceive the organisation versus the competition) but also to high levels of employee loyalty and satisfaction which derives from good internal relationships and working environment (internal service quality). This is shown in Figure 1.4.

Studies in Europe as well as the US show that to retain customers and maintain profitable growth, organisations need to ensure they have a large number of advocates for their business. It is only truly 'delighted' customers who remain loyal to the organisation. Customer satisfaction and delight is directly related to the experience the customer receives wherever and whenever they contact the organisation. The quality of external service delivery is a reflection of the quality of service that people within the organisation provide each other. Employee retention and satisfaction are essential to this. In particular, when employees do not feel valued or appreciated, they are less likely to deliver excellent internal or external service. Therefore the style of leadership that is demonstrated across the business determines the quality of the service experience. Figure 1.5 illustrates the elements in this chain in more detail.

This philosophy suggests that measuring internal customer satisfaction is as equally important as measuring external customer satisfaction. This is because the way in which different parts of an organisation interact with their internal customers has a direct impact on employee satisfaction (in particular the degree to which they feel valued by the organisation) and employee retention. This in turn influences external service quality, customer satisfaction and retention. Figure 1.5 illustrates the elements in creating profit and growth.

To gain an in-depth knowledge of the factors that dictate service quality, employee attitude surveys and internal customer audits should be an important part of an organisation's service strategy.

In general, businesses find that there is a correlation between internal customer satisfaction measures and external customer satisfaction measures. AT&T, for example, found that a 3 per cent increase in employee satisfaction related to a 1 per cent increase in customer satisfaction. There is often a time lag between an increase in employee satisfaction and the increase in customer satisfaction of between 6 and 18 months, but the correlation is always there.

Figure 1.6 is a chart from the automotive industry showing the highest and lowest scoring dealerships in terms of customer satisfaction. Overlaid are the two dealerships' employee satisfaction scores.

Furthermore, research by ISR, a consulting firm that specialises in measurement of employee opinion, shows that there is a link between employee satisfaction and a company's financial performance, so measuring employee satisfaction is a must. And again, a study conducted by People Management (April 2003) amongst Tesco stores demonstrated a clear difference in customer and employee satisfaction amongst stores with above average, average and poor levels of leadership.

USE RESEARCH TO ESTABLISH CUSTOMER LIFETIME VALUE

Equally, customer measurement will help your organisation determine the lifetime value of

Business imperative →	Internal service quality →	Employee satisfaction and retention →	Service value →	Customer satisfaction and retention →	Commercial success
Organisations need to have:	Elements that create good internal service are:	Elements that drive employee satisfaction and retention are:	Service value is visible through:	Customer retention is enhanced by:	Equates to:
Customer-focused mission and goals	The right tools for the job	Leaders who focus on the customer	Clear customer promise	Seamless service: management of total customer experience	Profit
Strategies to address competition, environment, global and local economy, technology and pace of change	Adequate resources	Leaders who promote excellent service	Product features	Listening and responding to customer needs and concerns	Shareholder value
	Effective and efficient systems	Clear direction setting (goals, service vision and customer promise)	Consistency / Reliability	How the service is delivered	Customer lifetime value – the longer customers remain with the organisation, the more profitable it becomes
	Appropriate structure	Open communication	Quality	Service recovery strategies when things go wrong	
	Appropriate job design	Appropriate employee selection and development	Value for money		Employee retention
	Relevant core competencies	Empowerment / Coaching	Loyalty programmes		Re-investment for the future
	Effective internal measures	Effective team building and management			
		Reward and recognition			

Figure 1.5 Creating profit and growth

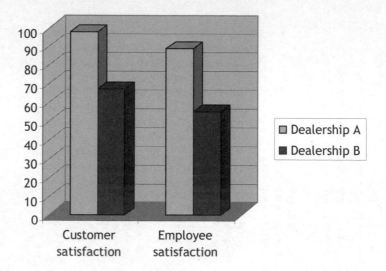

Figure 1.6   Comparison between top and bottom dealerships

customers. For example, in the automotive industry, the majority of customers in the UK change their cars on average every three years. As an example, say for every medium-sized car a dealer sells it makes £700 a sale, and may also expect in a three year period to make the same amount on servicing and parts. Research can determine the average age of the customer when they first purchase a particular make of car. It can also establish what percentage of customers remain loyal and the factors that determine loyalty. Therefore, say the average customer for a first-time purchase of a particular make and model of car is 35, they change their car every three years and they remain loyal until they are 50: then the lifetime value of the customer is $5 \times £1400 = £7000$.

This formula does not take into account the number of recommendations that loyal advocates of an organisation give to other people (again this can be established via research), so potentially the lifetime value of this customer is worth more than this.

Customer measurement will also help you establish the lifetime value of customers.

USE MEASUREMENT TO ENCOURAGE INNOVATION AND CONTINUOUS IMPROVEMENT

Becoming a customer-centred organisation is a journey without an end point, whose purpose is to keep meeting and exceeding customer expectations. Measurement is essential in enabling the organisation to establish a starting point for the journey to service excellence as well as giving it a road map of how the journey is progressing.

Customer feedback can be used to set service quality goals – both for internal as well as external customers. It can also be used to drive the establishment of:

- service level agreements
- service standards
- process improvement
- people development

- reward and recognition
- benchmarking inside and outside your organisation.

I discuss these service initiatives in more detail in Chapter 8.

By measuring on a continual basis and by effectively communicating and *acting* on the results, a culture of service excellence and continual improvement will be encouraged.

Timing your measurement

How often you measure needs to be given careful consideration and should be dictated by your customers' life-cycle and buying patterns as well as other external factors that may impact on customers' opinions and feelings. Measure too often and fatigue may occur: the findings of the research may not indicate significant change; you may have to wait for more time to pass before trends can emerge. There may not be enough time between research to effect changes and people may not take as much heed of the results of the feedback. On the other hand, leaving measurement to an annual event means that nearly a whole year can have passed before corrective action can be taken; employees will have to wait up to 12 months to receive feedback on what they have done well as well as areas for improvement.

In addition to ad hoc measurement to identify specific service issues, best practice appears to be a cycle of three- or six-monthly reporting with identification of trends on a cumulative basis. How often you measure needs to be a topic of discussion in the preparation phase of measuring service effectiveness – see Chapter 3. You may also choose to run a pilot survey to 'test the waters' rather than running a full scale one. Whatever interval you choose, the first and subsequent surveys should result in an index of customer satisfaction that will act as a benchmark of customer perceptions.

Assess your current approach to customer service measurement

Look at the following statements and assess your organisation:

Customer service measurement criteria	In place	Not applicable	Needs to be acted on or addressed
Improving customer satisfaction and retention is a key driver for our business.			
Our organisation has a service strategy and service measurement plays a key part in this.			

Customer service measurement criteria	In place	Not applicable	Needs to be acted on or addressed
Our leaders show their commitment to service excellence in words and in their behaviour.			
We have an effective service measurement system in place to listen to the voice of the internal as well as the external customer.			
The service measurement system in my organisation helps me assess our current performance in the eyes of our customers.			
The service measurement system we have in place sets the agenda for where we want to be as a service provider.			
Our service measurement system helps me monitor the progress of service initiatives and improvements.			
The service measurement system we use encourages continuous improvement.			

Customer service measurement criteria	In place	Not applicable	Needs to be acted on or addressed
The findings of current customer research are well communicated and acted upon.			

2 *Preparing to Measure Customer Service*

In this chapter you will find tips on:

- setting objectives for customer service measurement
- how to gain buy-in for measurement
- choosing the correct audience to gain feedback from
- selecting the best measurement techniques
- determining your sample size
- selecting external measurement providers.

Key questions to ask in the planning and preparation phase

As mentioned in Chapter 1, organisations spend vast amounts of money on customer service research that is then not acted upon. To ensure that this does not happen to you, here are some questions to ask as you plan and prepare to measure your service effectiveness:

1 What do you want to achieve from the research?
2 Who is the sponsor for the research?
3 What will you do with the results?
4 How would you like the information presented after the research takes place?
5 Who will be instrumental in acting upon the findings and how will you involve them in preparing and planning the research?

Here are some tips to consider in answer to each of these questions.

WHAT DO YOU WANT TO ACHIEVE FROM THE RESEARCH?

For example, do you want to identify areas for improvement in the service you provide, rate your service against your competitors or discover what percentage of customers are loyal to you?

A tip is to write clear and specific objectives that are measurable and time-bound. If you have an overall aim for the research, it is useful to break this down further into specific objectives. These should be written as outputs, using active verbs stating what you will be able to do by the end of the research.

For example:

Aim

To measure the level of satisfaction amongst customers who call or write to our organisation.

Objectives

By the end of the study the organisation will be able to:

- describe what is important to customers who call or write to our organisation;
- state the levels of customer satisfaction with our telephone and written responses;
- identify the key areas of improvement amongst customers who call or write to our organisation.

WHO IS THE SPONSOR FOR THE RESEARCH?

Identify someone in your organisation at senior management level who will take the role of sponsor, champion the research and have enough 'clout' to ensure that the findings are acted upon.

WHAT WILL YOU DO WITH THE RESULTS?

This may seem an odd question but what you want to do with the results of the service measurement may dictate the methodology you choose to measure service effectiveness and the way that you wish the information to be presented.

For example, if you wish to make comparisons on a unit by unit or department by department basis, this would call for quantitative research. If you wish to use the information to help your team better understand the feelings, opinions and emotions experienced by your customers, this may call for qualitative research.

How you intend to feedback the information and to whom, may also dictate the method used.

HOW WOULD YOU LIKE THE INFORMATION PRESENTED AFTER THE RESEARCH TAKES PLACE?

For example, bar charts, scatter diagrams, photographs, verbatim customer comments, video footage? This will help the production of the report.

WHO WILL BE INSTRUMENTAL IN ACTING UPON THE FINDINGS AND HOW WILL YOU INVOLVE THEM IN PREPARING AND PLANNING THE RESEARCH?

To gain 'buy-in' for the measurement, it is best to identify who will be involved in implementing the potential actions from the research and then consider how to involve them up-front in the planning and preparation phase. For example, should you form a small project team composed of yourself, your sponsor and representatives from service providers to manage the project? In order to overcome potential objections, early involvement is essential.

A stakeholder map (see Figure 2.1) can help identify who may help and hinder the project and strategies for involvement.

Name of person:
List their role in the project:
    Sponsor, team member, customer, supplier, adviser, other

List whether their view of the project is:

Positive
Neutral
Negative

List the person's degree of influence:

H = high
M = medium
L = low

List actions to influence the person towards having a more favourable view of the project.

Figure 2.1   Stakeholder map

Choosing the correct audience

To best measure service effectiveness it is important to ensure that the research is conducted amongst a representative sample of your customers at random.

Imagine every business as an orange made up of segments (Figure 2.2). Each segment represents a homogeneous customer group. Would all of the segments be the same size in terms of their value to your organisation? Probably not. In choosing the correct audience to gain feedback from, you need to consider how you segment the orange. A market segment consists of a group of individuals or organisations who, because they share one or more characteristics, have relatively similar product or service needs. Criteria commonly used to describe consumer markets are:

1 Geographical location of potential customers – country, region, urban, rural, and so on
2 Their demographic characteristics – age, sex, marital status, and so on
3 Socio-economic groups – social class, status, income, and so on
4 Psychological characteristics – attitude, motivators, life styles, and so on
5 The benefits that they seek from using the products or services
6 The amount of product or service they purchase or consume.

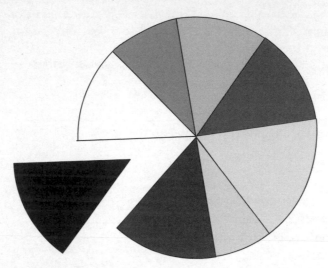

Figure 2.2   Segmenting your market

When identifying your audience for research, remember to include customers who have gone elsewhere or those who never shop with you or use your products and services.

In business to business markets many of the segmentation characteristics above apply though often consideration needs to be given to the market sector and the service delivered as well as the value of the customer's business.

Another key determinant is whether to include decision makers or influencers as well as users.

For example, one technology business to business client for whom I undertook customer research had clients in each of the following market sectors:

- life sciences
- health
- telecoms, media and networks
- financial services
- manufacturing
- energy and utilities
- consumer products, retail and distribution.

Its services ranged from outsourcing to strategy and transformation. Much of its business was gained at a senior management level. Typical decision makers were chief executive officers and finance directors. However, once the project was implemented the service provider had greater involvement with middle managers and more junior users within their clients' businesses.

In determining the audience for this service audit, I needed to ensure that my sample represented customers from each of the market sectors and all of the services offered on a nationwide basis. Typically 80 per cent of the organisations revenue was produced from 20 per cent of their client base. It was essential that the survey represented this fact. This was achieved by representing the value of the contracts won, whether large, medium sized or small, as well as representing decision makers and influencers at board, senior and more junior user levels. I also needed to include existing customers as well as customers who had not renewed their contract or who had decided not to award the service provider the business.

The public sector does present some particular challenges when measuring, given the legislative framework in which it works. In the health service for example, national service frameworks dictate the assessment that takes place in terms of standards of care.

The emphasis on public sector reform has been on consultation. One of the key considerations is the need to consult a wide variety of stakeholders when conducting research. For example when working on a survey in the primary care sector, I had to seek the views of the following people:

- patients using the practice
- clinical staff (doctors and nurses)
- practice staff
- primary care trust
- patients' association
- national patients' organisation
- local medical council
- community health workers
- social services
- local community interest groups.

It is helpful therefore, in any public sector research, to brainstorm all the people who need to be consulted or informed about the project. A 'RACI' diagram (Figure 2.3) is a useful aid here. RACI stands for:

Responsible: who will *do* the work
Accountable: the buck stops here
Consult: who you need to hold a two-way dialogue with
Inform: who you need to let know that the project is happening, for example one-way information

Another consideration is to ensure that you offer non-English speakers access to the measurement. It is a legal requirement to provide material in Welsh. The best practice is to offer other non-English speakers the opportunity of this facility in written form, on the phone as well as face to face.

Phase of the project	Person responsible	Person accountable	Consult	Inform

Figure 2.3   Example of RACI diagram

A further difficulty could be that some cultures are not familiar with giving feedback and may need encouragement to do so. Some measurement techniques may not appeal to certain groups so consultation is required during the exploratory phase of research to ensure that the methodology is inclusive.

The best practice is to ensure access to all, therefore arrangements may be required for people with special needs at public consultation sessions, focus groups and during other measurement sessions.

A further consideration is the Freedom of Information Act 2000. We recommend strongly that the results of all measurements are made freely available.

Selecting the best measurement techniques

Once you have agreed who you should include in your sample, you are in a position to select the best measurement techniques and determine the sample size to use to gain feedback.

Select the measurement methodology that best suits your target population. Questions to ask are:

- What are the objectives of the measurement?
- Who are the target population?
- In order to satisfy these objectives with this target population, do I need to obtain information that I can quantify or do I need views and opinions?
- Given the target audience, what methodology/ies is/are most suitable?

There are two main forms of customer measurement techniques: quantitative and qualitative.

Quantitative methods allow you to quantify opinions. They use fact-based methods to help identify satisfaction levels, improvement areas and trends. This involves using hard data as an objective means of making a judgement. The results of quantitative research methods can often be presented in percentage terms.

Qualitative methods allow you to understand customers' perceptions and experiences. They use expressive methods to help identify customers' views and opinions and the reasons behind them. The resultant data allows organisations to better understand the whys, hows and whats of customers' experiences.

Here are the main methods that fall under each category:

Quantitative methods:
Historical reviews
Postal and email questionnaires and surveys
Telephone surveys
Analysis of complaints and compliments
Customer comment cards and suggestion schemes
Mystery shopping
Structured interviews.

Qualitative methods:
Customer focus groups

One-to-one interviews
Free phone or free video point
Consumer-to-consumer online discussion forums or web-based focus groups
Conversations
Exploratory interviews.

There are advantages and disadvantages to each of these methods:

Advantages	Disadvantages
Historical reviews	
• Allow you to review data, measure and monitor trends	• May not be representative of current customer views
• Useful at beginning of research phase to help decide focus	• Review may be selective
	• Requires more follow up
Written questionnaires	
• Can reach a large amount of people	• Response rate can be low – on average 10 per cent therefore can be costly
• Provides quantitative data	• Difficult to obtain information on customer opinions
• Useful way of quantifying opinions expressed in customer interviews or focus groups	• Questionnaire can be designed from service provider perspective without reflecting what is important to the customer
Postal and email surveys	
• Can reach a large amount of people	• Can be considered as spam and a nuisance, therefore response rate can be low
• Provide answers to specific questions	• Difficult to obtain information on customer opinions
• Can provide instant results	• The longer the length of the survey, the lower the response rate
• Provide quantitative data	
• Useful way of contacting customers at a distance	
Telephone surveys	
• Provide instant response	• Many customers dislike intrusion
• Provide quantitative data	• Not easy to gain trust
• Useful way of contacting customers at a distance	• Difficult to elicit information on customer opinions
Analysis of complaints and compliments	
• Provides 'dip-stick test' of customer opinion	• Not representative of total customer opinion, only customers who have had 'magical' or 'miserable' experiences
• Can identify trends	
Structured interview	
• Gain customer responses face to face	• Requires skill in interviewing techniques
• Interviewer can explain intentions behind the questions	• Time consuming
	• Open to bias from interviewer
• Allows sample to be taken of customers – say every tenth customer who comes into the store throughout the day	• Structured nature of questions does not allow for in-depth discussion

Advantages	Disadvantages
Mystery shopping	
• Provides objective view of customer service	• Questions often formulated by the organisation not the customer, therefore can be biased
• Allows all units or service providers to be assessed using the same measures	• Can be seen as 'spying' by staff
• Highlights lack of consistency and training needs	• Low acceptance by staff of results – the mystery shopper is only one customer on one occasion and is therefore not representative of total customer experience
Customer focus groups	
• Allows organisation to explore customer opinions	• Needs good facilitation to ensure that all customers attending can give their opinions
• Allows in-depth discussion and frank feedback	• Not statistically valid
• Useful in exploring sensitive issues	• Does not allow opinions to be quantified. Data sometimes difficult to analyse
• Consultative and inclusive	
• Useful for gathering sensitive data	
• Helpful in exploring a range of views prior to using structured, quantitative methods	
One-to-one in-depth interviews	
• Allows organisation to explore customer opinions	• Time consuming
• Allows in-depth discussion	• Expensive
• Consultative and inclusive	• Not representative
• Useful for understanding opinions and feelings	• Not statistically valid
• Helpful in exploring a range of views prior to using structured, quantitative methods	• Can be influenced by interviewer
Free phone or video forum	
• Provide opportunity for customers to give feedback	• Not representative of total customer opinion, only customers who have had 'magical' or 'miserable' experiences may contact
• Demonstrates that the organisation cares	
• Can identify trends	
Consumer-to-consumer online discussion forums or web-based focus groups	
• Useful forum for customers to air views and opinions	• Not representative
• Agenda driven by customers	• Customers may air views and opinions you do not want other customers to know
Conversations with customers	
• Provide informal information	• Anecdotal, not representative
• Quick 'dip-stick' approach	• Open to bias and misinterpretation
Exploratory interviews	
• Useful to discover customer opinions prior to full-scale research study	• Expensive to set up and run
• Open-ended questions allow interviewer to explore customer's feelings as well as opinions	• Not representative of total customer group
• Interactive	• Time consuming

HOW TO ENSURE THAT YOU ARE USING THE RIGHT MEASUREMENT TECHNIQUES

As demonstrated above, each of the methods has both advantages and disadvantages – so how do you ensure that you are using the method that will get the best results?

Firstly consider which method is most suitable to your customers. Is it feasible for example to contact your consumers by email? How many of your customers have email and how do they consider its use?

Secondly consider a combination of both qualitative and quantitative techniques. For example, you could hold a series of customer focus groups to establish customers' opinions. Based on these findings you could then develop a questionnaire to be sent to a wider population in order to quantify the opinions.

You will find more about quantitative and qualitative research in Chapters 4 and 5.

Determining sample size

Once you have established your measurement methodology, you need to establish your sample size. How can you ensure that your research is clear, credible and impartial and properly reflects your customer base?

If you have a customer base of 75 000 people, do you need to speak to them all for your survey results to be correct? The answer is no; with a 5 per cent margin of accuracy you would only need to speak to 382 of your customers.

The main point to take away is that sample sizes are worked out using statistical formulae and do not work in proportion to each other. So for example if you had a population of 37 500 customers (half the size of the above) the sample size with a 5 per cent margin of error needed to be statistically valid is 380 people.

Population size	Number of respondents to be statistically accurate to 5% **margin of error** and **confidence level** of 95%
10 000	370
5000	357
2500	333
1000	278
500	217
250	151

There are some useful websites that help you calculate the sample sizes you need to be statistically accurate, for example www.surveysystem.com/sscalc.htm

To use these sites, you need to understand the basis on which sample size is calculated and in turn how to interpret results. This is important because using the correct sample size will save you money, time and effort. You may also have to defend the results of the research, particularly if the customer feedback is unpalatable or unexpected. In our experience one of the most common reasons for dismissing or disregarding the results is to pick holes in the sampling methodology, for example, by saying that the sample was not representative.

FORMULA FOR DETERMINING SAMPLE SIZE

For those of you with little inclination for mathematics, the following explanations may appear lengthy, but they are relevant to how you select your sample size and how you analyse survey results, so please bear with me. For those of you who employ research organisations to measure service effectiveness, hopefully this explanation will demystify some jargon and give you some pertinent questions to ask.

There is a mathematical formula that describes the sample size formula that you need to calculate. This is:

> The *error of margin* in a sample = 1 divided by the square root of the number of people in the sample.

This formula is derived from the **standard deviation** of the proportion of times that a researcher gets a sample 'right' given a number of samples.

STANDARD DEVIATION

The standard deviation is useful for those who measure customer service to know as it helps to identify the data that lies behind the average (or mean) scores often presented as part of research reports. It tells you how spread out the respondents' answers to your questions are in relation to the average. Why is this useful? Imagine you have received a report from an external research agency telling you that the average score that customers in the survey gave for 'responsiveness to their needs' was 5.5 out of 10. The average score hides the range of scores – some customers may have scored you 1 out of 10, others 10 – see the example shown in Figure 2.4. Therefore the average score alone does not indicate the deviation from the mean.

Score	1	2	3	4	5	6	7	8	9	10
Number of responses	15	15	0	0	0	0	0	0	15	15

Figure 2.4   Average score does not tell the whole truth

DISTRIBUTION CURVE

To understand the concept of standard deviation it is useful to consider the distribution curve, as shown in Figure 2.5.

The normal distribution curve illustrates the distribution of scores across a scale. So if we looked at car drivers in the UK the set of data we analysed would probably show that most car owners are close to the average (changing their car every three years) while relatively few examples tend to one extreme (changing their car every ten years) or the other (changing it every three months).

Most distribution curves are bell shaped, although some will have relatively steep curves, while others are relatively flat. Standard deviation is a statistic that tells you how tightly the respondents' answers are clustered around the mean. When the answers are bunched

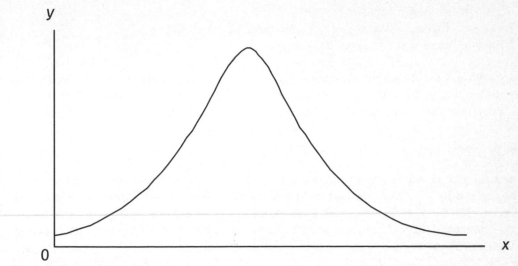

Figure 2.5   Distribution curve

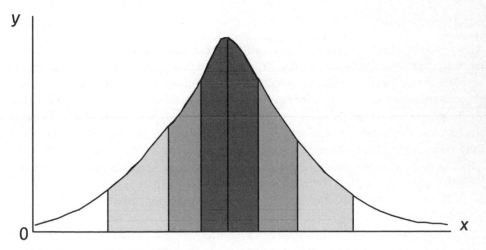

Figure 2.6   Example of standard deviation

together around the mean, the bell curve will be steep. When the answers are spread out the bell curve is relatively flat. As sample size increases the more likely it is that data collected will tend towards the norm.

Figure 2.6 is an example of how standard deviation works.

One standard variation (in the area in Figure 2.6) away from the mean in either direction on the horizontal axis accounts for around 68 per cent of people in the group who did not score the mean. Two standard variations from the mean (the dark grey areas) indicate 95 per cent of people did not score the mean. Three standard deviations (the dark grey, mid grey and light areas) indicate 99 per cent of people who did not give the same score as the mean.

If you want to calculate the standard deviation, either use a website, or the following formula:

x = one value in your set of data
Average (x) = the mean (average) of all values x in your set of data
n = the number of values x in your set of data

For each value x, subtract the overall average (x) from x, then multiply that result by itself to determine the square of the value. Add together the squared values. Then divide that result by (n–1). Find the square root of this number. This is the standard deviation of the data.

MARGIN OF ERROR

The **margin of accuracy or error** (sometimes called the **confidence interval**) is the line that is often inserted at the bottom of political polls. For example 'Labour has a lead of 10 per cent over the Conservatives with a plus or minus 3 per cent margin of error'. This means that when asked this question in a poll 100 times, 95 of those times the percentage of people giving an answer would be within 3 points higher or lower than that of the people who gave Labour a lead of 10 per cent in this pole. Therefore in 95 per cent of occasions the lead could be between 7 per cent (10 – 3) and 13 per cent (10 + 3).

CONFIDENCE LEVEL

Why 95 per cent? This is what statisticians call a **confidence level**. This is how sure you can be about the validity of the research. It is expressed as a percentage and represents how often the true percentage of the population would pick the same answer. With a confidence level of 95 per cent therefore, you can be confident of the research findings 19 times out of 20 but on the 20th occasion you may get a completely different answer. A 95 per cent confidence level means that you can be 95 per cent certain, a 99 per cent confidence level that you can be 99 per cent certain. Most researchers use a 95 per cent confidence level.

You can be most confident of the accuracy of your sample, the larger your sample is. This will mean that your margin of error (or confidence interval) decreases. However the relationship is not linear and doubling your sample size does not automatically halve the size of your margin of error.

The accuracy of the results of your service measurement is also affected by the proportion of respondents who answer a particular question. So if 51 per cent of respondents answer 'yes' and 49 per cent 'no', the chances of accuracy are far less than if 99 per cent of respondents answered 'yes' and 1 per cent answered 'no'. One well-known organisation changed its corporate image on the basis of a response split of 51 per cent in favour of the new logo and 49 per cent against. They went ahead with the changes but suffered subsequent unfavourable consumer comments in the press.

SAMPLING METHODS

The accuracy of customer measurement results is also affected by how random your sampling was. So, for example if you conducted a telephone survey to sample the customers of a utility company and only called customers during the day, your sample would be biased and not random.

There are three main types of sampling that you can use:

Random sampling

Here you select customers to be contacted as part of the research on a random basis. So if you wanted to select a random sample from a customer base of 1000 people, you would choose a series of numbers at random to contact, for example, the 9th, 19th, 29th, 39th, and so on, until you have a sufficient number. Some computer software packages such as Microsoft Excel allow you to enter your customer data and it will produce a random sample for you.

Stratified random sampling

This involves dividing your population into homogeneous subgroups and then taking a simple random sample in each subgroup. This ensures that you will be able to represent not only the overall population, but also key subgroups of the population, especially small minority groups.

Non-random sampling

Non-random sampling, because it is non-random, almost certainly introduces bias. It can be difficult to draw conclusions about the population based on information derived from a non-random sample, as samples are often *unrepresentative* of the population. So, for example, asking the first ten customers who walk through the door to take part in a customer survey will not be representative of the total customer base. Neither would asking the first ten customers who called your organisation that day. In the same way using complaints and compliments as a measure of customer service is a non-random sample and open to bias.

Generally speaking, it is best to work from sample sizes of at least 100 respondents (less than this and your data is not statistically valid). When sample sizes fall below 100, as is often the case with business to business customers or for sub-segments of your sample, the best practice is to use a mixture of qualitative (opinion) as well as quantitative (statistical) methodologies – see Chapter 3.

To work out how many questionnaires to send to customers, you have to have some idea of the anticipated response rate. So, if the response rate to postal questionnaires is 15 per cent and you need a sample of 151 to give an error margin of 5 per cent and a confidence level of 95 per cent, you would have to send out 1006 questionnaires to your customers (151 returns = 15 per cent, divide 151 by $(15 \times 100) = 1006$.)

Given the complexity of ensuring that the results of customer service measurement are valid and representative of your customer base, you may consider selecting an external provider to assist you in this process. The Market Research Society, based in London, is a useful source of information about research agencies that specialise in customer service measurement. Specialist market research agencies can handle the complexity of large scale research. They also provide a degree of authority and independence to a project. The British Airports Authority, for example, uses external resources to help it monitor customer satisfaction across its airport sites. It also uses external agencies to administer ad hoc surveys.

Agencies are also particularly useful when it comes to administering employee satisfaction and internal service quality surveys as they are independent and non-biased.

Whether you use an external agency or not, it is worth agreeing a time plan for the measurement with your sponsor. Also worthy of consideration is whether to pilot the research methodology to establish likely response rates and customers' reactions. In addition it is useful to develop and agree on a contingency plan with your sponsor in case response rates are low or customers are reluctant to take part in the measurement exercise.

Assess your current approach to preparing to measure customer service

Look at the following statements and assess your organisation:

Customer service measurement criteria	In place	Not applicable	Needs to be acted on or addressed
We have set clear objectives for our customer service measurement.			
We have a sponsor at senior level for the research.			
We have identified the target population for the research.			
We have selected measurement techniques that are relevant to our target customer.			
We use a combination of quantitative and qualitative research techniques.			
We have determined the correct sample size.			
We have determined the customers who will take part in our survey using random sampling.			

Customer service measurement criteria	In place	Not applicable	Needs to be acted on or addressed
We have determined the sample size needed by response rate.			
We have considered whether to use an external measurement provider.			
We know the standard deviation and confidence level of our research results.			

3 *Qualitative Customer Service Measurement Methods*

Qualitative methods for customer service measurement are a useful starting point for any research. They provide the organisation with a cross-section of views and opinions about the customer experience that can then be verified and substantiated using quantitative methods.

In this chapter we discuss:

- Exploratory research and its benefits
- What customer focus groups are and how they can be established
- Running a focus group
- The skills of facilitation
- Dealing with difficult situations in focus groups
- Projective techniques for focus groups
- Following up the results of focus groups
- Video, web-based and customer-to-customer focus groups
- Preparing and running one-to-one in-depth interviews
- Analysing the results of one-to-one interviews
- Other methods of qualitative research.

Exploratory research and its benefits

To ensure that the measures used to quantify the customer experience are those that are important to the customer rather than those that seem important to the organisation, it is essential to conduct exploratory research before a large scale survey is undertaken. Qualitative research methods allow exploration of customers' views and opinions and are the best way of determining the range of customer experiences. These can be gathered from current and lapsed customers as well as prospective customers. Once you have conducted exploratory qualitative research, you are in a better position to determine what measures are needed to provide quantitative hard data. Customer focus groups and in-depth one-to-one interviews are proven methods of exploratory research. We discuss both these methodologies in this chapter.

Customer focus groups

Customer focus groups are investigative research events where up to ten customers meet under the guidance of an expert facilitator to discuss their service experiences, their views, feelings and opinions in an open forum. Customer focus groups are a useful way of establishing a comprehensive range of opinions on customer values, assumptions and beliefs about the service you provide as well as looking at future service offerings and improvements. They are particularly helpful amongst consumer markets and can also be used in business to business environments. However, in some business-to-business environments they are not appropriate because of the potential of conflicts of interest amongst those customers attending. If the topic is non-controversial and not commercially sensitive, it is sometimes possible in a business setting to hold customer focus groups as part of company events.

It is normal practice to recruit customers for focus groups from amongst your existing customer base. Customer focus groups can also be conducted amongst lapsed users or those people who have never used your products or services. When recruiting for a focus group be sure to try to include customers who represent a wide range of opinions, for example, those who are delighted, indifferent and disappointed about your service. It is also helpful to consider whether you need to run a series of focus groups with homogeneous groups, for example some with light users, others with heavy users and so on.

There are three methods that are most used to recruit customers to a focus group:

1 Recruitment of customers on a volunteer basis, for example advertising for customers through in-store posters or on the website where appropriate. Nationwide Building Society has advertised for customers to attend a focus group in this fashion.
2 Recruitment by personal invitation, for example letter or personal invite. Lloyds TSB has taken this approach.
3 Recruitment by a market research agency. This is often useful where the organisation does not have a physical presence in the marketplace that is accessible to all customers.

When recruiting, there are some general rules that apply:

• Recruit customers three to four weeks before the expected customer focus group meeting so that they can put the date in their diaries.

• The optimum number of customers to recruit is ten. Any more than this and it is difficult for people to express their opinions.

• Send a letter to all those attending – see the example shown in Figure 3.1

• Expect one or two customers not to show up. It is worthwhile calling customers before the event to ensure that they are able to attend.

• Allow one and a half to two hours as the duration of the focus group.

• Select a venue that is central for customers to attend – some organisations hold customer focus groups in their own units, for example the AA used the opportunity to show customers round their control centre by holding the focus group there. Other organisations hold the groups in hotels or specially fitted out focus group centres where two-way mirrors allow members of the client organisation to view the proceedings without taking part. It is also possible to video focus groups with customers' permission so that members of the organisation can see the customers expressing their opinions.

• Provide refreshments. It is important that customers feel at ease throughout the session.

Dear xxx,

We are constantly striving as an organisation to improve the quality of service we provide. As a valued customer, I am delighted to invite you to a customer focus group meeting at xxx on Tuesday 13th April at 19.00.

The purpose of the customer focus group is for us to listen to your honest opinions on our service – what we do well, what we do not so well and where we can improve.

You will be joined on the evening by nine other customers. The focus group will be facilitated by an independent consultant and will last approximately one hour. Refreshments will be provided. As a gesture of our appreciation, we will pay you £35 at the end of the meeting.

Please return the form below in the reply paid envelope to indicate whether you are able to attend.

I hope to see you on 13th April.

Figure 3.1   Example of focus group letter of invitation

- Select a start time that is most suitable to your customers. For example, I have held business-to-business focus groups as 8.00 a.m. breakfast meetings and we have held focus groups at 6.30 p.m., 7.00 p.m. and 8.00 p.m. for consumer groups.

- Offer customers an incentive for attending (at the time of writing the average incentive is £35 per person for consumer groups). Explain that you will issue this at the end of the focus group (to save paying those people who do not turn up).

HOW MANY FOCUS GROUPS SHOULD YOU RUN?

The number of focus groups that you run will depend on the size of your audience and the geographical distribution of your customer base. In practice, I find that once the number of focus groups reaches between 8 and 12, the same generic themes emerge, though often with regional or unit specific variations. Focus groups are a tangible way of demonstrating to customers at a local level that they and their opinions are important to the organisation. Consideration should also be given therefore to how beneficial it will potentially be to run more focus groups in each location (or clusters of locations). We have often trained regional and area managers in facilitation skills, for example, so that they can run customer focus groups in their own and others' regions.

RUNNING A FOCUS GROUP

Key to the success of a focus group is careful preparation and effective facilitation by an independent moderator.

It is advisable to use a neutral facilitator to run customer groups in your own area. In practice it is difficult to remain neutral when customers are commenting on an area of operation in which you are directly involved.

When preparing for the group, consider the topics you wish to cover, the running order and how much time you have. Focus groups last on average between one and two hours depending on the number of topics to be covered.

Remember to turn up at least half an hour before the start time as some customers tend to arrive early.

Start the session with easy, non-controversial topics to get people to open up. It is better to cover general or generic issues before coming on to specifics. Throughout the focus group the facilitator should use open questions to encourage the focus group participants to speak.

Here is the running order for a simple focus group for a retail supermarket chain. The group is run by a neutral facilitator who is a representative of a different part of the organisation, and so can remain independent. You will see that the group is recorded with the permission of those attending. This is so that the facilitator can write notes up after the session. It is normal to tape record the session, although sometimes a video recorder can be used. There are also purpose-built focus group facilities where members of the organisation can view the discussion live as it happens without being seen. There are issues of confidentiality when it comes to recording or transmitting the sound and images subsequently so remember always to get customers written permission to do this. As a rule of thumb, all comments from focus groups are not directly attributed as it is an overview of opinions that you are seeking, rather than who exactly said what.

It is wise to have the minimum number of representatives (one or two) from the organisation present at the focus group meeting itself. If there are people from the business present their role should be to meet and greet. They then need to sit outside the group, observe and take notes. If there are any specific questions, they can speak to the relevant customer after the focus group to answer these. Importantly representatives from the organisation must be briefed not to participate in the focus group – it is the customer's views that count!

Example customer focus group running order

INTRODUCTION FROM FACILITATOR

- Welcome and thank customers for coming.

- Introduce yourself and your role. Explain that you will act as a neutral facilitator.

- Explain that the customer focus group is being held in an effort to improve the quality of service xxx provides.

- Explain that the discussion will last approximately one hour. Ask customers to please give their honest opinions as their views are important.

- Explain that you will be taking notes or recording the session (turn on tape recorder) so you have a record of their comments – check everyone is OK with this.

- Explain that there are other members of xxx management here sitting outside the group (introduce them). They will not take part in the discussions but can answer any specific questions at the end.

- Ask customers to introduce themselves by the name they would like to be called. Make a record of their names.

LEAD A DISCUSSION AROUND THE FOLLOWING TOPICS:

1 How often do you shop at xxx?
2 How long have you been a customer here?
3 What is important to you when you shop at xxx?
4 What do you particularly like about shopping at xxx? (Prompt reasons why.)
5 What do you think of the people working at xxx?
6 What frustrations or annoyances have you encountered in dealing with xxx?
7 What would you like to see xxx doing, which they are not?
8 What one aspect of our service should xxx change above all others? (Go round the group and ask each person.)

- Summarise discussions.
- Thank and close.
- Give out vouchers.

You will see from the running order above that typical customer focus group discussions centre around what is important to customers, what is going well, frustrations and annoyances and areas for improvement. As customers who attend focus groups can sometimes be outspoken, the facilitator needs to ensure that there is a balance of views and that what is going well is addressed as well as what should be improved. This involves making sure that everyone is included and summarising regularly to show that they have actively listened.

Questions should be asked about what customers expect of the service so that the organisation understands the desired service levels.

It is possible to ask one or two quantitative questions as part of focus groups to gauge general reactions, for example 'on a scale of one to ten (where 1 = low and 10 = high) provide an overall rating of your satisfaction with the service provided'. If you do ask customers to provide a rating it is best if this is a written one as well as verbal as members of the focus group can be swayed by others with strong opinions. Sometimes for example, focus group members can individually answer a short questionnaire as they arrive. This can be used as the basis of discussion and handed in at the end of the session.

THE SKILLS OF FACILITATION

The facilitator is highly influential in making the focus group run smoothly. Facilitation is the art of 'making things easy' (from the French word *facile*, easy).

It is advisable to use a trained facilitator to run the focus group. If there are none within your organisation, external companies can provide this service. A facilitator is neutral, and does not contribute to the discussion or evaluate what is being said, so do not pass comment or take sides. Facilitators are good listeners and use open and probing questions to guide the discussion. They encourage and allow everyone to speak.

At the start of the focus group the facilitator relaxes the group, speaks to every member of the group and makes sure that they all have a chance to introduce themselves in the first five minutes.

A key part of the skill of the facilitator is being aware of the process of the group – how people are interacting with each other and each person's percentage of airtime. The effective facilitator does not allow one person to dominate the group but asks everyone their views. Effective facilitators draw out quieter members of the group and are not afraid of silence. They summarise on a regular basis and make notes to show that they have taken on board what has been said. They are also aware of and skilled in techniques for dealing with difficult situations.

DEALING WITH DIFFICULT PARTICIPANTS

There are a number of situations which may present difficulties in focus groups. Bringing together eight to ten strangers can create many different dynamics and social pressures.

If there are members of the focus group who become particularly emotional or outspoken, the facilitator has a number of options available to them:

- Acknowledge the strength of opinion, feelings or emotion.
- Summarise the key points to show that they have actively listened.
- Ask what other people feel about the topic in an attempt to open up the discussion.
- Ask the customer to speak to the representative of the organisation in more depth at the end of the discussion (or to leave the group to do this if appropriate).
- Suggest that the group takes a short break for refreshments.
- Ask the customer to let other people speak so that you can record a balance of views.
- Divide the group into twos or threes and ask them to discuss their experiences, then take the views of each of the subgroups.

If the group is not very talkative and there are prolonged silences:

- Ask participants to write down the answers to the questions and collect these in.
- Introduce a projective technique (see below).
- Divide the group into twos or threes and ask them to discuss their experiences, then take the views of each of the subgroups. Participants may be reluctant to speak in front of people they do not know well.

If the group has either nothing to say that is positive about the organisation, or conversely nothing to say that is negative:

- Use examples of what other customers have said about the organisation to generate discussion, for example, 'A common complaint is ..., what are your experiences of this situation?'
- Use projective techniques to explore perceptions.

PROJECTIVE TECHNIQUES FOR FOCUS GROUPS

Projective techniques are methods that use visual imagery, drama, pictures and other creative tools to help customers express their views and opinions.

Here is a selection of projective techniques that can be used in focus groups:

1 Ask everyone to draw how they view the organisation as if it was a mode of transport such as a car or a boat. Then ask participants to show their pictures and the words they would use to describe them. Probe for the reasons why.

2 Ask group participants to think of three organisations that epitomise excellent service in their eyes. Allow them ten minutes to act out an example of excellent service from these three organisations and also an example of how the service in your organisation compares with this.

3 Ask the group to imagine that your organisation had the opportunity of extra funding. The investors are willing to fund two new areas for the business but in return the business has to get rid of one – what would these areas be?

4 Supply the group with magazines and newspapers. Ask them to cut out words and images that they associate with your organisation and the service it provides and to make a collage. After ten minutes ask the group to display the collage and talk through what it means.

5 Produce a list containing the names of your and other service organisations (some of which may be your competitors). Ask focus group participants to brainstorm the words that they associate with each company (see more on brainstorming in Chapter 7). Once you have captured the words, hold a discussion around the reasons people have given for these.

6 Ask the group to imagine that a fairy godmother has waved a magic wand and has made all the group's wishes about the organisation come true. Ask them to brainstorm what they are now seeing in this future state as customers that is different to what they are seeing now, what they are hearing, what they are feeling and what they are saying.

7 Ask the group to describe their ideal supplier and the characteristics they associate with them. Then ask the group to rank your own organisation against these criteria. Probe for reasons for the rankings and identify areas and priorities for improvement.

FOLLOWING UP THE RESULTS OF FOCUS GROUPS

Once the focus group has finished, there are a number of actions the facilitator needs to take:

• Write up notes from the customer focus group and circulate these to the appropriate people. Include key phrases and verbatim remarks used to express feelings and mood.

• Analyse the data and look for trends – break the data down into issues which need to be addressed at a unit or regional level and generic, organisational issues.

- Identify emerging themes at a generic level.

- If the focus group has been site specific there may well be general issues that need to be fed back to head office as well as improvement issues specific to the location.

- Discuss and agree specific improvement actions.

- If location-specific, inform members of staff about the discussion topics and the improvement actions.

- Publicise the results of the focus group to customers – for example Asda puts large posters in the entrance of its stores letting customers know the improvement actions it has taken based on listening to their feedback.

VIDEO, WEB-BASED AND CUSTOMER-TO-CUSTOMER FOCUS GROUPS

The popularity of focus groups has meant that variations are now run using new media options. For example, I have seen business-to-business focus groups run using video conferencing. I have also facilitated focus groups that have been videoed. The subsequent film of the customer discussions was shown to employees throughout the organisation starting with the board. The impact was dramatic. For the first time the voice of the customer was heard and seen throughout the organisation. In many ways my experience is that the visual impact of seeing customers express their views is far more powerful than reading a report or listening to taped transcripts of customer research. The emotion expressed by customers is often a call to action to the organisation.

Likewise the web is now being used to host, albeit written, customer focus groups where customers join an open forum to discuss their views. First Direct has extended this concept. They sent out 30 000 emails asking their customers just what they thought about them. They received 1061 replies. They subsequently interviewed and filmed 14 respondents. The comments from these customers formed part of their advertisements and on their website the same customers speak for themselves.

First Direct have recognised the potential of customer-to-customer endorsement. Analysts predict that this will be a growing trend. They envisage that a prospective customer will pay more credence to existing customers and their service experience than the advertising an organisation presents to attract new business. An interesting question to ask during web focus groups for example is, 'What sorts of questions should a prospective customer ask an existing customer to decide whether to use their services?'

One car manufacturer found that existing customers are most likely to recommend a particular marque if they are recent customers rather than long-standing ones. It is worth investigating therefore which customers are most likely to recommend your services.

Another approach is to develop a community feel to your website so that customers become part of a loyal club. Online retailer handbag.com has developed discussion groups on their website. Customers exchange tips on a range of topics such as health and fitness, careers and finances. Their dwell-time on the site is ten times greater than that of the equivalent chat room.

Many organisations have suffered from the negative impact of poor customer experiences when disgruntled customers have set up parody websites to express their anger and frustrations, such as a site called Un-tied Airlines instead of United Airlines. In the US there is also a site called Wal-Mart Sucks.

To guard against negative customer comments being broadcast, it is well worth therefore encouraging feedback and customer focus groups on your own organisation's website. Shell, who have on occasions been criticised by some groups on environmental issues, set up a bulletin board called 'Tell Shell'. The site welcomed feedback and was unfiltered so it contained both fierce criticism as well as favourable opinions.

Increasingly as technology develops, organisations need to be aware of and adopt alternative means of communicating with their customers, albeit with their permission. Witness the rise of text messaging and interactive TV – more votes were polled for the TV series *Big Brother* than in the general election!

One-to-one in-depth interviews

Another form of qualitative feedback is in-depth one-to-one interviews. These can take place as part of exploratory research as well as a stand-alone methodology.

In-depth interviews take place in both consumer and business markets. Often because of their cost, they are mainly used in business-to-business environments. As this is an expensive option, this methodology is often confined to key customers or key customer groups.

In a business environment the difficulty of one-to-one interviews is finding a time when everybody is free, particularly because the discussion can last several hours. Therefore it is advisable for the customers' key contacts in the organisation to contact them personally to explain the importance of the research and to gain the customers' agreement to participate. As with focus groups, it is advisable that the person who services the account is not present during the interview so that the customers can really open up and express their true opinions.

It is advisable to use an expert interviewer to conduct in-depth one-to-one research. The quality of the output of the discussion is dependent on the ability of the interviewer to create rapport with the customer, to probe and identify underlying feelings and nuances. The interviewer needs to establish at the beginning of the interview whether the comments can be attributed or not or whether they need to be treated in confidence.

If it is not cost-effective to employ the services of an expert interviewer, when using internal interviewers ensure that they have the ability to:

• build rapport with the interviewee;
• remain neutral;
• use open and probing questions;
• listen actively;
• record outputs accurately.

IN-DEPTH INTERVIEWS AS PART OF EXPLORATORY RESEARCH

When using in-depth interviews as part of exploratory research, the interviewer needs to work from a blank canvas, that is, the interviewee drives and sets the agenda, rather than the interviewer. In practice this means that the interviewer's aim is to discover what is important to the customer when using the products or services of the organisation. The interviewer writes down the list of attributes that the customer describes, making note of the ones that the customer says first. Coming to mind first, these attributes are usually the ones that the customer considers most important.

Next, the researcher asks the customer to rank the attributes in order of importance. By undertaking this process with a small sample of customers and asking them to rank the outputs, the researcher builds up a picture of what is important to customers and therefore, which questions to ask and in what order during subsequent research. You will note that the interview is driven by the customer, it is not advisable for the researcher to prompt using a pre-prepared list of attributes as this means the organisation has pre-conceived ideas of what should be included in the research.

To conclude the exploratory research the interviewer then elicits the customer's views about how well or otherwise the organisation meets these expectations. The interviewer uses the list of importance attributes as a discussion guide for this part of the interview, for example, 'You said that of primary importance to you was dealing with helpful staff, what are your views on how xxx organisation performs against this criteria?' In reality the interviewer will use the information gained on importance ratings to build the subsequent research questions, rather than the customer's responses about satisfaction levels. However, to conclude the interview, the researcher needs to prompt around both areas.

SEMI-STRUCTURED AND STRUCTURED INTERVIEWS

When using in-depth interviews as part of the research process after exploratory research, the interviewee can adopt a semi-structured or structured approach. With a structured approach, as with focus groups, the interviewer can ask a mixture of open and scalar questions. These are questions that allow the respondent to rate different items on a scale, for example, of agreement, importance or satisfaction. Importantly, the interviewer needs to probe the reason for responses, particularly to scalar questions.

Using a semi-structured interview approach, the interviewer has a list of topic areas to cover (derived from the exploratory research). The interviewer prompts using open questions to encourage the customer to provide opinions on the topic areas and probes to discover underlying reasons and feelings. The interviewer also encourages the customer to raise topics which are important and is prepared to 'go off piste', that is, abandon the order of the intended interview if the customer has an important issue to raise.

Whether using a structured or semi-structured approach, the interviewer needs to create a good rapport with the customer and show that he or she is actively listening and capturing the customer's views. To aid this process, it is helpful if the interview is taped, but only with the consent of the customer. In sensitive situations many customers may refuse this request, in which case excellent note-taking is called for.

The interviewer needs to establish as part of the introductions the purpose of the research, how the results will be used and whether the customer wishes their comments to be attributed or not. Some customers may wish to air their views in confidence.

During the interview, although the interviewer has questions to ask, these are prompts for discussion and to draw the customer out. The interviewer needs to be an effective listener, to build on what the customer has to say and probe further, for example, 'You said earlier that the sales person needs to have the support of the rest of the organisation; what do you think about the support that your sales contact receives from xxx?'

Once the interview has been completed, the customer needs to be thanked and, as with all customer service measurement, be kept informed about actions that will be taken as a result.

Here is an example of a semi-structured business to business in-depth interview that looked at the initial contact with the client through to the servicing of the account. The questions are prompts for the interviewer to elicit the customer's opinion and probe further.

Example of in-depth interview questions in the business-to-business market

INTRODUCTION

Explain who you are, the purpose of the research and how it will be used. Explain when the results will be published. Clarify whether or not the customer wishes to give their comments in confidence.

FIRST CONTACTS

- How did you first hear about xxx (name of organisation)?
- What was your perception of xxx prior to the commencement of the procurement process?
- On what basis was this perception formed?
- Why was xxx selected as a potential supplier?

THE PROCUREMENT PROCESS

- What is important to you when you deal with suppliers during the procurement process?
- What do you think in general of the way xxx acted during the procurement process?
- What were xxx's strengths during the procurement process?
- And what were their weaknesses?
- How long did the procurement process take?
- Did the length of the procurement process meet your expectations?
- If appropriate, how could xxx have made the process faster?

THE SERVICE OFFER

- How relevant was xxx's service offer to your business needs?
- What is your view of xxx's strengths in terms of service offer?
- What in your view are the weaknesses of the service offer?

THE PROPOSAL

- How relevant were xxx's proposals to your needs?
- How competitively priced was the proposal in relation to what you were expecting?

THE SALES PERSON

- What adjectives would you use to describe the xxx sales person?
- To what extent do you feel that the sales person has the support of the rest of xxx?
- How would you describe the liaison between sales and delivery?

THE CONTRACTUAL PROCESS

- How easy was the contractual process to take part in?
- What do you think of the length of time the contractual process takes?

FOLLOW-UP TO REQUESTS

- How promptly does xxx follow up your requests?
- How pro-active are xxx in managing your business?

THE COMPETITION

- How would you characterise your dealings with xxx versus your dealings with the competition?
- What are xxx better at compared with their competitors?
- What are xxx worse at compared with their competitors?

THE FUTURE

- What would lead you to buy from xxx again?
- What are the key areas that xxx needs to improve?

THE STUDY

- What do you think about taking part in the study?
- How could the study be improved?
- What else would you like to add that has not been covered in the questions above?

Thank the interviewee. Confirm how the results will be used and when.

ANALYSING IN-DEPTH INTERVIEW RESULTS

The results of one-to-one interviews can be used in the same way as those for focus groups to identify what is working well and what needs to be improved on an individual (or account-specific) basis. The results can also be used to identify trends and commonly held views and opinions by comparing and contrasting the data.

Owing to the very nature of unstructured interviews, it often takes time to draw out patterns and trends. If the sponsor of the research is keen to have this data, it is helpful to include some quantitative questions as part of the research in order for direct comparison and conclusions to be made, for example, 'On a scale of 1 to 10 (where 1 = low and 10 high), what rating do you give to the organisation's responsiveness to your requests?'

In Chapter 7, I discuss presenting results. As with focus groups the results of the research come to life when you include verbatim remarks.

Other methods of qualitative research

There is a general move towards using qualitative research methodologies to supplement quantitative methods as they are perceived as more customer friendly and interactive. In addition they allow the research to be driven by the customer rather than the organisation.

Businesses are now investing in other innovative methods of qualitative research. British Airways, for example, set up video booths in their departure and arrivals lounges so that customers could express their comments live to camera. Other organisations are using chat room facilities and online and face-to-face forums to gather customer comments.

Assess your current approach to using qualitative customer service measurement methods

Look at the following statements and assess your organisation:

Customer service measurement criteria	In place	Not applicable	Needs to be acted on or addressed
We use exploratory research to ensure our measurement is driven by what is important to the customer.			
We use qualitative as well as quantitative research methods to gather customer feedback.			
Our organisation runs customer focus groups.			
We use in-depth one-to-one interviews in our business as a means of tracking key customer satisfaction.			
We offer facilities on our website for customers to tell us their views.			
We have established networks so that customers can meet and chat to other customers.			

Customer service measurement criteria	In place	Not applicable	Needs to be acted on or addressed
We have other innovative means of gaining qualitative feedback from customers in place.			

4 *Quantitative Research Methods*

Frederick F. Reichheld, guru of the loyalty industry is quoted as saying: 'I've given up on satisfaction surveys. They don't work.' (www.eCustomerServiceWorld.com). His two books on loyalty, *The loyalty effect* (Harvard Business School Press, Boston,1996) and *Loyalty rules* (Harvard Business School Press, Boston, 2001), have spawned a greater focus on customer loyalty as a driver of profit and growth.

The six most common mistakes in customer research according to Reichheld are:

1 asking too many questions;
2 surveying the wrong customers;
3 inappropriate timing and frequency;
4 lack of responsibility within the organisation for acting on the results;
5 not working through the consequences of the findings;
6 inadequate 'gaming safeguards' so people can work the system to produce favourable results.

In this chapter we look at ways of creating meaningful measures of customer satisfaction and adapting these measures to methods such as:

• postal and email questionnaires and surveys;
• telephone surveys;
• structured interviews;
• customer comment cards and suggestion schemes;
• mystery shopping;
• analysis of complaints and compliments;
• observation.

These techniques can be used in conjunction with qualitative methods to gain a rounded viewpoint of customer satisfaction.

In the health service, one organisation arranged surveys and focus group meetings amongst people with special needs and non-English speaking customers to assess its accessibility. It sought volunteers from amongst this population to act as mystery shoppers. Their role was to phone, email, fax, write and visit the organisation and assess how they were treated against given criteria. The results were very surprising to the organisation, which until then had no objective measures of its service in this area. This prompted the development of a special needs improvement plan so that the requirements of this sector of the population were catered for.

Designing a questionnaire

When designing a questionnaire, many people make the mistake of making it too long, uninteresting and not customer-focused. Another big mistake is focusing on customer satisfaction scores rather than comparing customer satisfaction levels against their expectations of the service they receive.

The results of the survey are therefore not helpful to the organisation: they may be giving the wrong message or may not be easy to interpret. The resulting actions may be difficult to prioritise.

The best practice when designing a questionnaire is to ask questions about what is important to the customer, and then to ask questions around their satisfaction levels. Asking questions about importance helps clarify what customers expect of different aspects of your service.

Why use the term importance and not expectations? Studies have shown that importance is a more valid indicator than expectations. For example, customers often have low expectations of service. It is easier to rate importance – this equates to expectations.

If you just ask customers alone to rate their satisfaction, you receive a different picture than if you ask them to rate both satisfaction and importance.

For example, one training consultancy asked its customers to rate their satisfaction with the service they provided. They received the results shown in Figure 4.1 (using a scale of 1 to 10 where 1 = low and 10 = high).

Item	Satisfaction (score out of 10)
Training venue	6
Quality of accommodation	5
Food	7
Quality of training material	6
Tutor's content knowledge	8
Tutor's rapport with delegates	9
Tutor's encouragement and support	8
Tutor's presentation skills	7

Figure 4.1   Training customer satisfaction levels

Looking at this list, it appears that the quality of accommodation is the aspect of the service with which clients are least satisfied. It is therefore the area that the organisation would give most priority for improvement. Other areas for improvement are the training venue and the quality of the training material.

However, looking at this information from a different perspective by asking customers to rate the importance of aspects of the service before they rank their satisfaction, a different picture occurs as shown in Figure 4.2.

Item	Importance (score out of 10)	Satisfaction (score out of 10)	Gap analysis
Training venue	6	6	-
Quality of accommodation	6	5	-1
Food	9	7	-2
Quality of training material	6	6	-
Tutor's content knowledge	10	8	-2
Tutor's rapport with delegates	8	9	+1
Tutor's encouragement and support	8	8	-
Tutor's presentation skills	9	7	-2

Figure 4.2   Training customer expectations versus satisfaction levels

In this scenario customers have been asked to first rate the importance of different aspects of the service they receive before they rate their satisfaction levels. By subtracting the score customers give for satisfaction from the score that they give for importance, thereby producing a gap analysis, different priorities for improvement emerge.

Here the biggest gaps in customers' expectations are the tutor's content knowledge and presentation skills and the food (gaps of -2). The next area for improvement in terms of priority is the quality of accommodation (gap of -1).

This is a very different result from that obtained as part of the first survey. This methodology also helps to identify areas where the organisation also *exceeds* expectations (for example the tutor's rapport with the delegates is +1). It prevents an organisation seeking higher satisfaction for things that customers do not view as important.

CUSTOMER DELIGHT AND RETENTION VERSUS SATISFACTION

Using importance versus satisfaction ratings is one way of assessing customers' delight with your product and services. Why delight? In the US, an organisation called the American Customer Satisfaction Index (ACSI) tracks customer satisfaction on an annual basis. It, like other organisations of its kind, found that satisfaction scores are not linked to sales growth. K-Mart is an example of this: high customer satisfaction score and no growth. So, just because customers are satisfied with your service does not mean that they will buy more from you or recommend you to their friends.

Potentially the satisfaction surveys on which organisations spend so much time and money are a weak tool in terms of measuring whether customers will be loyal to you, and therefore whether you are being effective in terms of your service offering. A better measure is customer loyalty: do customers remain with you, spend more with you and recommend you to their friends?

Reichheld has shown that it costs between five and nine times more to gain a new customer than it does to keep an existing one. A 5 per cent increase in customer retention can lead to 20–125 per cent increase in profit.

CUSTOMER RELATIONSHIP MANAGEMENT

Customer relationship management (CRM) is the name given to systems based tools that measure the type and quality of relationship that an organisation has with its customers. By collating information about the transactions a customer has had with the organisation in the past and its current dealings with the organisation, CRM systems enable the organisation to:

- gather customer data quickly;
- identify the most profitable customers over time;
- predict buying habits and patterns;
- increase customer loyalty by identifying opportunities to 'up-sell' and 'cross-sell';
- reduce the cost of servicing these customers.

Driven by the desire to form one to one relationships with customers, CRM aims to segment customer groups by their actual and potential value and target them.

Over the past years companies have invested large amounts in CRM, although a recent report by research group Gartner found that 70 per cent of implementations fail. Nevertheless, European companies were expected to spend a further £5.7bn on CRM in 2003.

The problem is that CRM is often driven by technology at the expense of people. The Gallup Organisation found that consumers rate people as the most important determinant of customer loyalty to brands. Customers have different types of loyalties to a company (see below), and not all of them want a relationship with suppliers.

Retention itself is also hard to measure, even with sophisticated CRM systems. There are degrees of loyalty: in banking for example, customers who are dissatisfied with their service often shrink their account balance and usage but still retain their account.

LOYALTY LADDER

Research agency The Leadership Factor indicate that there is a scale of loyalty to an organisation:

- Monopoly: for example, I have to fly from London to Nimes, there is only one airline that flies directly to this route and I am not prepared to drive, take a train or transfer to and from another airport.
- Apathy: for example, I have had my account with the same bank since I was 18. Inertia makes me leave my account open there.
- Incentivised: for example, I buy my petrol at BP because I receive points on my loyalty card when I do so.
- Convenience: for example, I shop at Marks and Spencer Food stores because it is on my way home from work.
- Advocacy: for example, I go out of my way to purchase from Pret A Manger in preference to other sandwich shops and I recommend them to other people.

LOYALTY QUESTIONS

In addition to including importance as well as satisfaction measures in your research, it is helpful to include a measure of loyalty.

Reichheld studied 14 cases and the one effective question linked most consistently to loyalty was: 'Would you recommend our organisation to a friend?'

Another approach is to turn what is a hypothetical question: 'Would you recommend our organisation to a friend?' into one based on experience, for example, 'Have you ever recommended our organisation to a friend?'

An alternative is to ask a question about repeat purchase: 'Would you choose to purchase from us again if you could turn the clock back?'

Andy Taylor, chief executive officer of Enterprise Rent-a-Car in the US believes that there is only one measure of loyalty: 'Get customers to come back for more and tell their friends.'

He and his team determined one question that links to repeat purchase: 'Were you completely happy with your rental?' Rental customers are polled by telephone; the response rate is 70–80 per cent. This is the only question that customers are asked and staff are graded according to the response. Taylor only promotes on customer votes so anyone who does not appear in the top group does not get promotion.

Natwest, in their postal surveys, use the loyalty question:

If you were asked to recommend a bank to someone who was considering opening a bank account, how likely would you be to recommend the branch where your account is held?

Very likely	Quite likely	Not very likely	Not at all likely

Barclays Bank use a 'magical and miserable' rating to measure their service effectiveness. Customers are asked questions to identify whether they have received poor service or whether they have been delighted by the service. The subsequent responses are factored to produce an index.

USE OF EXPLORATORY RESEARCH

The question that Enterprise Rent-a-Car generated for their customers works well for them as does the Barclays' index. Are the questions you use in your research meaningful? Have they been generated by your customers? Exploratory research can help here, as described in Chapter 3. For your research to be credible and valid, it is vital that the questions you ask are meaningful to customers and that they cover the attributes of service that are important to them.

We know of one organisation that placed great emphasis in their measurement on the customer being greeted within 30 seconds of entering the store. They trained their staff to stand at the door and greet customers; a large percentage of the store bonus was aligned to achieving the 30 seconds greeting.

Although stores followed this rule and customers indicated via postal surveys that the greeting happened, there was no resulting increase in sales and growth. During subsequent qualitative research discussions and customer focus groups it became clear that the vast majority of customers felt intimidated by the 30 second rule. Although they wanted to deal with friendly and helpful staff, they wanted time to consider the merchandise, rather than being 'pounced on' by staff.

Remember to use qualitative techniques to identify what is really important to your customers and to design your questionnaire around these attributes, rather than what you think is important. Be wary of using the same questions on a repeated basis without checking, by using qualitative research, that these questions are still meaningful to customers – expectations do change over time. We came across one organisation that measured, on an annual basis, speed of response to telephone calls when 15 per cent of its customer base had transferred their enquiries to the internet.

Postal and email questionnaires and surveys

Below are some useful tips when designing a printed questionnaire:

* Ensure that the questionnaire is easy to complete.

* Make the layout of the questionnaire attractive and appealing to the eye. Use plenty of white space and a type size of at least 12 points so that it is easy to see and follow.

* Use plain English so that the wording is clear to all, for example, say 'the car owner' not 'the keeper of the registered vehicle'.

* Explain the benefits of completing the questionnaire in the introduction and state why the organisation wants to hear customers' views.

* Reassure the customer that the responses will be treated in confidence.

* Make it clear what will happen to the results.

* Make the instructions for completion short and to the point.

* Include a reply paid envelope or return email address.

* Use questions generated from exploratory research by customers in customers' language – avoid jargon.

* Lay the questions out in a logical sequence so that it makes sense to the customer, for example don't ask about whether the service provider showed empathy and under-standing of the problem before the question regarding how easy the organisation was to contact.

* Start the questionnaire with easy questions that the customer can answer quickly.

* Make sure the questions and answers match.

- If you need to ask more personal details of the customer, such as, age or profession, put these questions at the end of the survey.

- Do not make the survey too long – response rates drop the longer the questionnaire is.

- Decide what type of questions you will ask the respondent:
    - Fixed answers: for example, 'Is it a good idea? Yes or No.'
    - Multiple choice: for example, 'Which word best describes this?' followed by a range of options.
    - Free choice: for example, 'Tick as many words as appropriate to describe…'
    - Open-ended questions: for example, 'Please list your reasons.'
    - Ranking: for example, 'Rank your preferred choice in order of preference.'
    - Rating: for example, 'Spread the 10 points over the words you prefer.'

- Don't use double-barrelled questions, for example, 'Did the sales representative take your details and did they tell you their name?' These should be two questions not one.

- Don't be biased in the questions you use, for example, 'Do we offer average or good service?' This pre-supposes that the service was not poor.

- Don't use leading questions, for example, 'Would you agree that it is more convenient to be transferred automatically to the advisor?' rather than, 'Is it more convenient to be transferred automatically to the advisor?' as the former style of questioning leads the customer to answer 'Yes'.

- Avoid ambiguous words such as frequent, often and many – you may have a perception of what these words mean which is different to that of the customer, for example how often is 'often'?

- Randomise the order of your questions so that the customer has to think of the response. When completing a questionnaire, subconsciously the respondent follows a pattern. It's best to change the order of responses especially if the questionnaire is long, so that the customer does not follow a pattern and give the same responses each time.

- Once you have asked questions about different service attributes, it is helpful to ask the customer to rate the overall performance of the organisation – this provides an index of customer satisfaction that can be measured on an on-going basis, for example:

    Overall, how satisfied have you been over the last six months with the service you've received from the branch you have visited most often?

Very satisfied	Fairly satisfied	Neither satisfied nor dissatisfied	Fairly dissatisfied	Very dissatisfied

- If you decide (as we recommend you do) to measure customer expectation against satisfaction using importance versus satisfaction ratings as explained at the beginning of this chapter on page 44, we advise that you ask questions on satisfaction *before* you ask customers to rate the importance of the service attributes. In other words, focus on the organisation's performance first before looking separately at customer expectations.

- Remember to allow space for additional qualitative comments. A useful tip is to ask customers to summarise what they like and dislike about the service. This is part of a W H Smith survey:
  1 Thinking about the service you received from staff on this occasion could you state all that you liked about it, if anything?
  2 And could you please state all that you disliked about the service you received at W H Smith on this occasion, if anything?

- Pilot the questionnaire with a small sample of customers before sending it to your entire target audience so that you can identify any potential problems.

- Be conscious of customers with special needs and make arrangements so that they are not excluded from responding.

- Select an appropriate time to send out the questionnaire. Avoid busy periods such as summer holidays or Christmas as you will receive a lower response rate.

- Think about how you will analyse the questions before you send out the survey.

RESPONSE SCALES

In postal, email and telephone surveys, the organisation has to decide the type of responses it anticipates that the customer will make. These need to be pre-determined, to allow data to be collated and analysed in a systematic fashion.

There are a number of different options when it comes to response scales. Below are a number of different possible approaches with my experiences of each.

Verbal scales

In these, respondents are offered a choice of verbal responses for example:

Completely dissatisfied
Quite dissatisfied
Neither dissatisfied or satisfied
Quite satisfied
Completely satisfied.

This type of attitudinal response option is called the Likert scale. Each respondent is asked to rate each item on some response scale. For instance, respondents could rate each item on a 1-to-5 response scale where:

1 = strongly disagree
2 = disagree
3 = undecided

4 = agree

5 = strongly agree.

There are a variety of possible response scales (for example, 1-to-7, 1-to-9 and 0-to-4). All of these odd-numbered scales have a middle value, which is often labelled 'neutral' or 'undecided'.

If you decide to use this type of scale, be sure to have an equal balance of positive and negative responses, for example:

very unhappy

quite unhappy

neither happy nor unhappy

quite happy

very happy.

As in the rest of the questionnaire design, be sure to use descriptors that the customer would also use. Be wary of biasing the results by offering only one negative option, for example:

poor

neither poor nor good

good

excellent.

Using an unbalanced scale such as this, organisations can claim to have 95 per cent satisfaction ratings, that is, 95 per cent of respondents scored neither poor nor good, good and excellent. This is not representative of the customers' true feelings and can lead to a false sense of security when customers are in effect going elsewhere.

The other problem to watch out for is the 'bunching effect'. If you have only four or five options, most respondents are likely to select the option 'neither good nor bad' or the option 'quite good'. It is not typical to see many responses at either end of the scale. There is quite a big difference for example in the response 'good' and 'excellent'.

If you do wish to use a verbal scale, we recommend using one that has seven options, for example:

very dissatisfied

dissatisfied

somewhat dissatisfied

neither satisfied nor dissatisfied

somewhat satisfied

satisfied

very satisfied.

One telecommunications organisation has used a nine point verbal scale:

dismayed

very dissatisfied

dissatisfied

somewhat dissatisfied
neither satisfied nor dissatisfied
somewhat satisfied
satisfied
very satisfied
delighted.

This allows the respondent more options and helps spread the range of scores.

It is also possible to use a forced-choice response scale with an even number of responses and no middle neutral or undecided choice. In this situation, the respondent is forced to decide whether they lean more towards the agree or disagree end of the scale for each item.

Note: On the telephone, the problem with all verbal scales is that they can be difficult for the respondent to grasp immediately and they often have to be repeated.

Numerical scales

Using numerical scales customers are asked to rate service attributes within a given range of figures, for example on a scale of 1 to 5.

Give careful consideration to the choice of scale; if you ask people to rate on a scale of 1 to 5 they go invariably for the middle box. Again, using this method, results usually fall between scores of 3 and 4. As a typical example, organisations average satisfaction scores will be say 3.75. Some people dismiss the 5 point scale therefore because effectively you end up using a 2 point scale (scores of 3 and 4).

The same caveats apply when you convert verbal scales, such as the Likert scale to numerical scales, for example:

very unhappy   = 1
quite unhappy   = 2
neither happy or unhappy   = 3
quite happy   = 4
very happy   = 5

The resulting average scores are likely to fall between 3 and 4.

In my experience it is better to use a 10 point scale (where 1 = low and 10 = high) to describe levels of satisfaction and importance than any other scale. Respondents (probably because of their experiences at school) are likely to give a score of 6 or 7 as average, a 9 for very good and anything 5 or below will be considered as poor. The resulting data is spread over a wide range (usually scores range between 5 and 9, given that people rarely score 10 and are less likely to score 1 to 4), and the data is also more easy to manage and interpret. Also, if this scale is used on a regular basis, my experience is that movements in importance and satisfaction ratings are more apparent than when using a 5 point scale, as shown in Figure 4.3.

An alternative to a scale of 1 to 10 is a scale of 1 to 6. This avoids the problems with the middle box.

Finally, do remember to include the option 'can't remember/have insufficient information', especially if you are asking people to recall a service that they received some time ago. Alternatively, put a note in the instructions to ask people who do not know the response not to complete the relevant questions.

	First quarter	Second quarter	Third quarter average score
10 point scale	7.4	7.8	7.6
versus			
5 point scale	3.7	3.9	3.8

Figure 4.3 Differences between 10 and 5 point scales

Thank you for using the services of our workshop. In order to ensure we meet your needs, please give us your thoughts on how we dealt with you. If you cannot remember or the question is not relevant, please leave this blank.

How would you rate the workshop on the following points, <u>thinking of this last visit</u>?

10   9   8   7   6   5   4   3   2   1

Completely   →   Completely
satisfied   dissatisfied

Score

Ease of getting service appointment within a reasonable time _____

Handling of telephone enquiries _____

Workshop opening hours _____

The waiting time at reception when leaving your car _____

Appearance of the service department _____

Friendliness and helpfulness at reception _____

The willingness and helpfulness of personnel to understand your problems _____

Value for money _____

If you have rated 6 or below, please list briefly, the reasons why:

Thank you for your help

Figure 4.4 Questionnaire using 1 to 10 rating scale and assessing satisfaction

EXAMPLES OF POSTAL SURVEYS

Figures 4.4, 4.5 and 4.6 show some examples of typical postal surveys.

Here are some examples of questionnaires that are not effective. The first one (Figure 4.7) does not provide a rating scale, therefore if sent out to a large number of customers the replies would be difficult to analyse.

The second questionnaire (Figure 4.8) uses a three point scale – excellent, good and poor. This questionnaire will result in biased results as it is only giving customers three options for response. There is a wide difference between 'excellent' and 'good' and between 'good' and 'poor'.

Patient questionnaire

We value your opinion on the quality of our customer care. Your views help us get it right.

To offer you the best possible service, we need to know what you think about what we do.

You don't have to give your name, so it's all **completely confidential**

Simply tick one box to give your opinion of each statement. If you agree strongly, tick box 5. If you disagree strongly, tick box 1. If your opinion is somewhere in between, tick boxes 4, 3 or 2, as appropriate.

	Strongly agree 5	4	3	2	Strongly disagree 1
Our practice opening times					
1. The practice opening hours and days are convenient	☐	☐	☐	☐	☐
How could they be improved?					

....

Our reception and waiting room					
2. The reception area is welcoming.	☐	☐	☐	☐	☐
3. The reception staff are friendly and helpful.	☐	☐	☐	☐	☐
4. The reception staff provide the information I need.	☐	☐	☐	☐	☐
5. The waiting room is nicely decorated.	☐	☐	☐	☐	☐
6. The posters and pictures are pleasant.	☐	☐	☐	☐	☐
7. The seating is comfortable and well arranged.	☐	☐	☐	☐	☐
8. There is a good selection of magazines available.	☐	☐	☐	☐	☐
9. The room is clean and tidy.	☐	☐	☐	☐	☐
10. The room is pleasant and relaxing.	☐	☐	☐	☐	☐
Your dentist and the treatment you receive					
11. I can talk to my dentist in an open way.	☐	☐	☐	☐	☐
12. My dentist listens carefully to what I say.	☐	☐	☐	☐	☐
13. My dentist explains about my treatment	☐	☐	☐	☐	☐
14. We discuss the different treatment options.	☐	☐	☐	☐	☐
15. My dentist gives me advice on dental care at home.	☐	☐	☐	☐	☐
16. The advice my dentist gives me is easy to follow and carry out.	☐	☐	☐	☐	☐
17. My dentist keeps pain and discomfort to a minimum.	☐	☐	☐	☐	☐

Finally
How could we improve our service to you?

....

Thank you for your help.

Figure 4.5   Example of dental practice postal questionnaire using a Likert scale

RESPONSE RATES

When using postal or email questionnaires to measure customer service, you can anticipate a response in the region of 10–20 per cent. The response rate will be better:

- if the topic of the survey is of particular interest to the customer;
- if the letter accompanying the survey is addressed in person and sent by a named representative of the organisation;

Thinking about your dealings with the branch, please select the option that best describes your opinion:

1. Do the staff:

Always go out of their way to make you feel welcome?

Generally treat you in an attentive and courteous manner?

Behave courteously but do not seem interested in you?

Make you feel that you are being a nuisance?

2. When using our counter service, of the available till positions are there:

Always enough open to deal with the number of customers?

Generally enough open to deal with the number of customers?

Often insufficient tills open to deal with the number of customers?

Always insufficient tills open?

3. Is the cashpoint service at your branch:

Always in working order?

Usually working but occasionally out of order?

Often out of order?

Totally unreliable?

Figure 4.6   Part of a survey using multiple choice questions

- if you use an incentive to encourage response (for example, entry to a free prize draw or first 100 questionnaires returned receive a free prize);
- if you publicise the survey in your outlets or on the website or if representatives of the organisation remind customers about the survey;
- if the survey is not too long – I recommend no more than four pages of questions;
- if you follow up with a reminder letter two to three weeks after the initial survey has been sent asking customers to complete the survey;
- if you tell respondents that you will publish the findings of the research (perhaps by posting them on your organisation's website).

Be prepared for respondents to include unsolicited comments on the questionnaire relating to their service experiences. One of our clients who sent out postal questionnaires for the first time was overwhelmed by the number of additional comments, queries and complaints contained within the responses, but made a personal commitment to respond to each one. When the organisation wanted to hold focus groups on a local basis they contacted a sample of the customers who had replied to the questionnaire. Later surveys asked customers whether they would be willing to take part in forthcoming focus groups.

As a valued customer, please tell us how you feel about the standard of our products, services and facilities?	
Product choice and availability	
Product quality and freshness	
Value for money	
Friendliness and helpfulness of staff	
Speed of service	
Car parking	
Any other comments	

Name:
Address:

Postcode
Telephone number:

Would you like to join one of our customer focus groups to discuss your views?

Yes ☐   No ☐

Figure 4.7   Postal survey using open questions

When using the internet as a survey mechanism, studies have shown that response rates are higher when the recipient receives a personalised invitation to respond. The difficulty with surveys sent over the internet is that they can often be treated as spam, so the more individual, interesting and involving the email, the higher the response rate.

It is usual for a link to the survey (see Figure 4.9) to be offered to the customer by email, as in 'click here to respond'. The best practice is also to offer a real-time alert if assistance is

Our aim is to recognise, respond to and exceed customers' expectations with enthusiasm.

To this end please give your assessment of the following areas by ticking one box.

HOTEL RECEPTION	Excellent	Good	Poor
Efficiency when making your booking	☐	☐	☐
Warm welcome, eager to please	☐	☐	☐
Service	☐	☐	☐

Comments ....
....

BEDROOM	Excellent	Good	Poor
Overall cleanliness	☐	☐	☐
Standards of facilities	☐	☐	☐
Comfort	☐	☐	☐

Are there any additional facilities/improvements you would like to suggest?
....
....

Comments..
....

Figure 4.8   Survey using a biased response scale

Feedback

We are already planning the conference for next year and whilst we asked for feedback during this year's event, you could help us further by taking part in our online feedback survey. The survey is designed to be completed in just 2-3 minutes and will help us to improve the event for 2004. Please take the time to provide your views by going to the following link: http://ecsw.surveylab.co.uk/.

Figure 4.9   The European Conference on Customer Management's invitation to online survey

needed in completing the survey. The organisation can then call or email the customer to provide assistance.

The major benefit of online surveys is that the system can be designed to offer continuous, real-time reporting. This means that as soon as a customer enters a response the results are updated accordingly. To ensure a high response rate, once the customer has competed the survey many organisations offer immediate access to the results.

Telephone surveys

The advantage of telephone surveys is that the response rate is higher than postal or email questionnaires. Typical response rates vary from 60 to 80 per cent.

One of the disadvantages, however, of telephone surveys is that in practice the length of the survey can be no more than ten to fifteen minutes.

Here are some tips on making telephone surveys:

- Use professional, courteous people to make the calls. They need to be patient too – some people view telephone surveys as a nuisance and may be reluctant to take part.

- Ensure that the interviewers are impartial – we have heard of cases where customers have had 'words put in their mouths' and others where the customer has been pre-advised by the sales person what to score so that the outlet (a retailer) met its targets for customer satisfaction.

- Time the call so that it is as near as possible to the time the customer has experienced the service. Kwikfit in the automotive industry, for example, phone a percentage of people each day across all their repair centres and ask them for feedback about the service they have received.

- Pay careful consideration to how often you call the customer – for example if you have a large customer base and you conduct a quarterly phone survey, it is wise not to contact the same customers each quarter for their opinions – apart from the nuisance factor, the sample will not be representative.

- Consider whether it is worth notifying customers beforehand that someone representing your organisation will call – this increases likelihood of response.

- If you are conducting a business telephone survey it is advisable to book a time for the call in advance.

- When making the call, ensure that the interviewer introduces him or herself and your organisation and states the purpose of the call, as well as explaining what will happen to the results of the survey and how long it will take (see Figure 4.10).

- If the timing of the call is not convenient to the customer, arrange an alternative time to phone.

- Ensure that the structure of the interview is simple to follow – remember that the customer does not have visual prompts.

- Use a rating system such as a scale of 1 to 10 as it saves time having to repeat the rating scales.

Ask for customer by name

'Hello, my name is XXX and I represent XXX (name of organisation). We are conducting a survey to find out about what customers think about the service we provide so that we can make improvements for our customers in the future. Do you have ten minutes to spare to answer a few questions? If not, when would be convenient to call back?'

Figure 4.10   Example of introduction to telephone survey

- If the customer scores 5 or below, prompt for brief reasons why they have given this score.

- Log the responses as the interview progresses – many research agencies have the script and questions on the screen in front of them so that they can type in the response in real time. If you do not have this facility, complete the questionnaire as you go along and write up any notes before you go to the next call.

- At the end of the call remember to thank the customer.

- If the customer has raised an issue that needs attention, ensure that this information is passed immediately to the person concerned and acted upon.

Face-to-face structured interviews

Another form of quantitative research is face-to-face structured interviews. Typically these take place in the outlets of an organisation, on the street, at people's places of work or in their own homes. I discussed qualitative interview techniques in Chapter 3. With structured interviews the interviewer guides the customer or potential customer through a series of questions. The agenda has been very much set by the organisation beforehand and there is little opportunity for the interviewer to probe in much depth.

This methodology can be expensive and relies upon expert interviewing techniques to attract the correct respondents and ensure that the results are not biased by the interviewer.

As with qualitative research, the empathy that the interviewer creates with the respondent is important. One retailer with whom I work encourages its departmental managers to conduct structured face-to-face interviews with customers in their department each month. Initially many of the managers were reluctant to do this but with training and guidance they discovered a huge benefit in listening to customers in an empathetic way. The lessons they learned from this exercise were:

- Rehearse how you will approach customers and what you will say to introduce yourself.
- Have a well-structured questionnaire prepared but if the customer wants to talk about something that is not one of your questions, follow the customer's lead; do not ignore the point.
- Don't justify or make excuses if the customer tells you something negative.
- Take immediate corrective action if the customer has had a negative experience.

- Write notes when you are with the customer as this shows you are listening.
- Remember to thank the customer.

Little Chef trained serving staff to conduct face-to-face interviews in its restaurants. They approached customers when they had finished their meals and asked them to rate the food, environment and service. Again after some initial scepticism, it found that it had a higher response rate and more balanced feedback on its service than relying on the customer comment books in each restaurant.

A typical running order of a face to face structured interview which generally lasts five to ten minutes is as follows:

- welcome
- introduction and purpose of the interview
- explanation of what will happen to the data
- guide the customer through the questions, noting their responses
- prompt where appropriate and probe using open questions for more detail, for example 'Tell me more', 'What exactly happened?', 'What else?'
- thank the customer
- close.

The interviewer needs to remember to use open body language throughout the discussion to put the customer at ease. Interviewers also need to show they are actively listening to create a relaxed atmosphere and demonstrate to customers that their views count.

One of the difficulties of face-to-face structured interviews is that 'catching customers on the hop' means that they may not have time to give a considered response. One option where time permits is to leave a questionnaire for the customer to complete, and then have the interviewer return and discuss the answers.

Customer comment cards and suggestion schemes

Customer comment cards and suggestion schemes have the major benefit of providing the customer with the opportunity to give feedback instantly. As a quantitative research method they are not sound because only customers with strong opinions – positive or negative – are likely to complete the cards. They do however serve a useful benefit in showing customers that the organisation is interested in their views.

If you are going to adopt this method, do ensure that it is not the only mechanism you use for listening to customers. Keep the cards simple and easy to complete, like the examples shown in Figures 4.11 and 4.12.

Where the customer leaves an address or telephone number, put in place a mechanism for acknowledging this. DIY specialist Homebase, for example, makes a point of contacting customers to address their concerns.

Even better, encourage customers to hand comment cards or suggestions to a member of staff. In this way if they have an issue or concern it can be addressed straight away. A caveat here; if you adopt this approach, do ensure that employees are trained in how to deal effectively with complaints so that the organisation can LEARN from the experience:

We would appreciate your comments, as these will help us in our efforts to constantly improve the level of service to you.				

What did you come to buy today?

....

....

How would you rate the following (please tick the appropriate box):

	Absolutely fabulous	Pretty good	Not bad	Mildly annoying	Truly dreadful
The ease of finding the products you wanted					
The speed and efficiency of our staff					
The product knowledge of our staff					
The attitude of our staff					

Would you recommend us to a friend?   Yes ☐   No ☐

Date and time of your visit: ....

Your comments and suggestions:

....

....

....

If you would like a reply from our store manager, please complete the details below:

Name:

Address:

Postcode: Telephone number:

Please post you comment card in the comment box behind the checkouts. Thank you for your time!

Figure 4.11   Example of comment card

Listen – Hear the customer out. Do not interrupt or justify.
Empathise – Show the customer that you appreciate their concerns.
Ask questions – Use open questions to establish the facts.
React – Say what you *can* do to rectify the situation. Focus on a positive solution.
Notify – the customer of what will happen next and other parts of the organisation, as appropriate.

In a serious attempt to improve our service to you, I'd be extremely grateful if you'd spend a couple of minutes filling in this short questionnaire. Our aim is to give you the very best service, because by doing so we hope you'll recommend us to others and be a customer for life.

Please help us by giving your frank answers to a few simple questions because it is only by listening to what you say that we can improve our standards.

If the service you received was good then I'd like to hear about it, if it has not been up to scratch in any way I need to hear about it.

I will be seeing all your replies and comments so please do tell me what you think.

Thank you for your help.

Figure 4.12   Example of introduction to comment card

Make sure that all customer complaints are acknowledged and dealt with whether in person or in writing. Hi-fi retailer Richer Sounds, the most profitable retailer per square foot in the UK, ensures that feedback forms are seen by owner Julian Richer in person and discussed in depth by Richer Sound's marketing team.

Mystery shopping

Mystery shopping is one of the most-used techniques for measuring customer service. In my opinion it has its place as a customer service measurement technique but not if it is the only form of measurement.

Mystery shopping allows the organisation to monitor the standards of service it provides across all parts of the organisation. Often used by retailers and in call centres, the technique measures the service during one transaction on one day normally with one service provider. People posing as real customers visit each outlet and subsequently record the quality of the service they receive against a set of criteria (see Figure 4.13).

Mystery shop criteria	Yes Score 2	No Score 0
Did the sales assistant acknowledge you?		
Was the sales assistant friendly?		
Was the sales assistant polite?		
Did the sales assistant take your order correctly?		

Figure 4.13   Example of criteria for a retail mystery shop

In some instances, people acting as mystery shoppers hide a tiny camera about their person. This records the transaction or enquiry they make with the service provider. The recording can then be played back later to the individual and manager to identify training needs.

When mystery shopping is used well the customer determines the criteria used to measure a business's customer service. All too often we find organisations using a long list of criteria to assess their units that has been generated by head office or regional managers. The mystery shop criteria do not reflect what is important to the customer; effectively the business is measuring what they want to pay attention to.

This only compounds the negative reactions that can often accompany mystery shopping:

'They are spying on us.'
'It was only one visit.'
'It's not representative of our true customers' experiences.'
'With a real customer I'm not normally like this.'
'We were very busy.'
'I knew it was a mystery shopper so I didn't bother.'
'They're time wasters.'

The excuses and justifications are particularly strong when bonuses are linked to mystery shopping, which is often the case. Some organisations such as sandwich chain Pret A Manger do succeed in operating a simple system, driven by customer needs and well accepted by employees. Each week every one of its outlets is visited. If the service the mystery shopper receives meets the measures set, the mystery shopper instantly hands the service provider a £50 reward.

Other organisations such as branches of John Lewis send their staff to mystery shop other stores in the chain. This is in addition to mystery shopping that is carried out annually by an external organisation. The thought is that it not only provides staff the opportunity of understanding and applying the measure to a sister branch but also increases their awareness of the needs of the customer.

If you do use staff or external agents to act as customers during a mystery shop exercise, you do need to ensure that they reflect your customer profile. They also need training in how to assess and score against the criteria and monitoring to ensure they apply this.

Organisations such as restaurant chain Pizza Express invite their customers to be mystery shoppers. They complete a questionnaire following their visit to a restaurant and mail it to Head Office. In return they receive a £10 Pizza Express voucher.

Mystery shopping is a technique that can also be used in competitive situations to assess competitive outlets' standards of service. It can also be used internally as we will see in the next chapter. If you do decide to adopt this form of measurement, I strongly advise that the criteria used are developed with customers as part of exploratory research. I also recommend that this is not the sole form of measurement of customer service that you adopt.

Financial services organisation Nationwide for example created a customer measurement system linked to branch bonuses. Each branch's customers' opinions were sought using postal questionnaires, customer focus groups and comment cards.

As well as mystery shopping. each element of the research had a weighted score. The total added up to 100 per cent. In this way Nationwide attempted to generate a balanced view of customer service rather than relying on one method alone.

Analysis of complaints and compliments

Surprisingly many organisations still use the analysis of complaints and compliments as the sole method of measuring customer service. Like comment cards and suggestion schemes, people who write in with complaints or compliments tend to be the minority, rather than the majority.

A study by research organisation TARP showed that 96 per cent of people do not bother to complain; they take their business elsewhere and tell other people (the suggested ratio is that you tell 5 people about a good experience and 11 people about a poor experience). Therefore the complaints that organisations receive are the tip of the iceberg. Likewise the number of people that recognise good service is low.

When people do complain, they are increasingly frustrated by how their complaints are dealt with according to a report by the Institute of Customer Service and human resources Consultancy TMI (*National Complaints Culture Survey 2003*).

My strong recommendation is to use the analysis of complaints and compliments as historical data that can highlight trends. It is important to analyse the root causes of complaints and address these. It is equally important to acknowledge and recognise an individual who has been complimented by a customer. However, to use complaints and compliments as the sole measure of customer service is not valid and could even be dangerous if the organisation does not receive many complaints.

Surprisingly, because complaint letters often go to the chief executive, it is one anecdotal way that the chief executive might use when assessing the strength of customers' feelings. (My consultancy often gets invited in by chief executive officers when they see an increase in the number of complaints.) In fact, in a customer-focused organisation, complaints should be actively encouraged.

One way of doing this is to encourage feedback in surveys on whether customers have complained or 'have felt like complaining' in order to identify areas of concern. Figure 4.14 is an example of this type of question from a bank's customer survey.

Have you complained or felt like complaining about the service you have received from us in the last six months? If so what was it about? *Please use both columns, if appropriate.*		
	Have actually complained	*Felt like complaining*
Bank in general		
Bank does not keep me informed, e.g. of charges		
Charges are too high		
Poor understanding of customer needs		
Too pushy about offering me things I don't need		
Cash machines not working		
Lack of cash machines available		

Figure 4.14   Questions about complaints contained in a postal survey

> Dear customer,
>
> We're sorry you found it necessary to return your order. But maybe we can learn something from your return and make a better product in the future.
>
> We've credited your charge card with the amount shown on the opposite side of this card.
>
> Again, sorry you had to make a return. If you have any questions, please call us free of charge on 0800 220 106.

Figure 4.15   Example of Landmark's proactive approach

Another way, is to anticipate situations that may cause customers concern. The breakdown service, RAC, promises specific response times to its customers; if it knows that it has failed to deliver these, it sends out a letter of apology, irrespective of whether the customer has complained.

Mail-order company, Landmark, also takes a proactive approach to complaints. Every time a customer returns an item the business sends a card, as illustrated in Figure 4.15.

Observation

The final quantitative method that can be used to measure customer service is observation. I do not mean this in the sense of observing customers per se. This method involves identifying a set of criteria and observing a customer *transaction* using the criteria as a measure.

Hotel chain Le Meridien developed a metrics and measures programme designed to measure and improve the quality of the service that it provided. It took key 'moments of truth', activities of critical importance to the customer such as check-in, and measured each component: average time to register, average number of people involved in the transaction, average time for baggage to arrive at the guest's room, and so on. In observing and timing each element as well as involving staff in identifying blockages in the process, the organisation managed to identify key areas for improvement as well as making comparisons and sharing learning across hotels.

TRY OUT DIFFERENT METHODS

In summary, to measure customer service effectively, a holistic approach is needed. Do not rely on one methodology alone to gather data, rather use and combine different techniques: What do the results of mystery shopping tell you that are different to postal or internet surveys? How do customer focus groups expand the information you receive from customer complaints? And so on. The key to success in measurement is setting up as many 'listening posts' as possible.

Assess your current approach to using quantitative customer service measurement methods

Look at the following statements and assess your organisation:

Customer service measurement criteria	In place	Not applicable	Needs to be acted on or addressed
We measure both importance and satisfaction as part of our research.			
We include a loyalty question in our quantitative research.			
We ask customers to give us an overall score for our service.			
We use both postal and email surveys to gather customer opinion.			
Our response scales are unbiased and appropriate.			
We use telephone surveys and face-to-face structured interviews where appropriate.			
We use comment cards and suggestion schemes to promote feedback from customers.			

Customer service measurement criteria	In place	Not applicable	Needs to be acted on or addressed
Our employees are trained how to handle complaints.			
We actively encourage complaints and compliments.			
We anticipate customer problems and take a proactive approach to them.			
Where we use mystery shopping, the measurement criteria are determined by the customer.			
We use observation of customer processes to measure customer service.			
We use a combination of different methods to measure customer service.			

5 *Measuring Internal Service Quality*

'Everyone is a customer, everyone has a customer.'

In this chapter we discuss:

- what is internal service quality and why it is important to measure this;
- measuring internal service quality at an individual, departmental and organisational level.

What is internal service quality?

In Chapter 1 I introduced the concept of the chain of events that links satisfied employees to customer satisfaction. This model, developed by Professors Heskett, Sasser and Schlesinger at the Harvard Business School, suggests that the quality of internal service dictates the quality of external customer service, as shown in Figure 5.1.

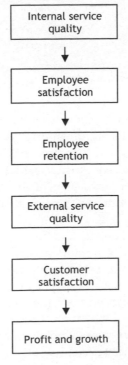

Figure 5.1   Internal and external service quality

(For a fuller description of the elements in this chain see Figure 1.5 in Chapter 1)

Many organisations spend time and effort measuring external customer perception without recognising that this is often a reflection of what is happening internally between individuals and departments. When you look at a typical service business you will see a number of functions that provide a service for one another.

In the example shown in Figure 5.2, the marketing, human resources, finance, information technology, facilities and legal departments provide a service to operations who in turn support both the sales department and the end customer. Each department has internal customers, only a few departments (sales and operations) deal directly with external customers.

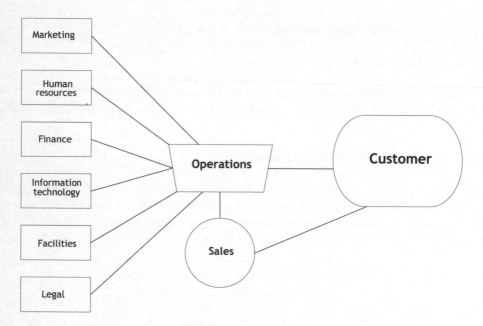

Figure 5.2   Each function provides a service to others

Typically in service organisations the people who have most contact with the customer are the ones who have the lowest status and who are the lowest paid. In a customer-focused organisation the pyramid is inverted. It is recognised that the heads of the functions and their management teams provide a service to and fashion the way in which service providers work for the customer. Each layer of management in turn offers a service to their internal customers: their team members. In this way the typical organisational pyramid is reversed as Figure 5.3 illustrates.

Unless internal service quality issues are addressed, an organisation will not be able to improve its external service quality or sustain growth and profitability. Measuring internal service quality at individual, team or department and organisational levels help identify factors that both help and hinder the attainment of service excellence as well as sending powerful messages across the organisation that internal as well as external customer service is important.

Research by ISR (www.isrsurveys.com) demonstrates that companies which – compared with the industry in which they operate – achieve above average financial performance also have higher levels of internal employee satisfaction and commitment.

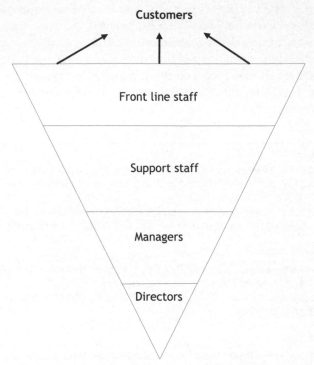

Figure 5.3   Inverting the organisational pyramid

These high performing organisations were characterised by:

- leaders who lead from the front and who care about their employees;
- an obsession with quality and innovation;
- putting the customer first, both internally and externally;
- a healthy culture where the organisation is seen to act with integrity, both internally and externally;
- investment in employees, including opportunities for growth and development as well as recognition for a job well done.

In a study by The American Society for Training & Development, those companies with higher net sales per employee, gross profits per employee and highest shareholder value spent highest on training per employee.

Part of achieving a culture of service excellence, therefore is ensuring that measures are in place internally to monitor service orientation at individual, departmental and organisational levels.

Measuring individual service orientation

How service orientated are your employees? Is customer focus a behaviour that the organisation truly values?

Those organisations that are truly customer-focused ensure that customer orientation is a key competency that employees throughout all levels of the organisation need to demonstrate. Competencies are the skills, behaviours and knowledge that people need to do their jobs well. They describe what is expected of individuals in different levels of jobs.

Figure 5.4 shows the customer focus competencies for three levels of jobs in one financial service organisation. Level 3 refers to the manager's role, Level 2 to the team leader's role and Level 1 to a team member.

Level 3
- Sets up and keeps in place multiple ways of gathering customer feedback across the business and uses this continually to improve products and services.
- Creates an environment that builds customer confidence by encouraging others to deliver beyond customer expectations.

Level 2
- Uses internal and external customer feedback to define and develop new and improved services to meet customer needs.
- Designs and implements processes and procedures that are truly customer focused.

Level 1
- Actively seeks internal and external customer feedback as the basis for measuring the level of service provided.
- Demonstrates excellent customer service personally.

Figure 5.4   Example of part of a set of customer focus competencies

A complementary approach to using a competency-based model is where organisations develop a set of values or behaviour codes that drive and dictate the way people operate throughout the organisation.

For example, my consultancy's values are:

Customer focus: We place high value on adding value to our clients, on meeting their needs and delivering excellent service.

Partnering: We place high importance on building close, long-term relationships that are both supportive and challenging. We work collaboratively to find a way forward rather than to impose our own solutions.

Learning: We place a high value in continuing to learn and develop, and we encourage others to do the same.

Integrity: We keep our promises, and are open, honest and fair.

Passion: We work in areas and use approaches that we have energy for and are passionate about; we encourage others to do the same.

Diversity: We work with a diversity of consultants, clients and approaches, to increase the opportunities for creativity. We work from the basis that people generally want to be and do their best.

These values underpin the way everyone in my consultancy goes about their business.

Insurance company Chubb's values are empathy, experience, fairness and promptness. They use these values as the basis of measuring the customer's experience.

The benefits of developing service-orientated values and competencies is that they provide a framework against which employees can be recruited, measured and developed. When recruiting new employees to his organisation Herb Kellher, chief executive officer of SouthWest Airlines, the only consistently profitable airline in the US, is quoted as saying: 'You can train skills, you can't train attitude.' Both SouthWest customers and existing employees take part in the hiring process for the airline. They have been known to turn down well qualified pilots as candidates because they did not have the necessary customer-service orientation on which the airline prides itself.

At sandwich chain, Pret A Manger, candidates work a shift with their prospective team and team members have the final say whether the individual demonstrates the behaviours that would make them a Pret person and therefore whether they will form part of their team.

Best practice service organisations measure a potential recruit's service orientation as part of the recruitment process. This can be part of a competency-based interview where recruiters seek evidence of the candidate demonstrating the required behaviours. Likewise, it is possible to measure how well a candidate's values match those of your own organisation.

Figure 5.5 is an example of questions that one organisation asks to establish potential candidates' customer orientation during recruitment.

- Who do you consider to be your customer in your current job?

- Can you give us an example of a time when you put yourself out to help a customer?

- Describe a situation where your customer was particularly pleased with something you did? Why was the customer pleased?

- Describe a time when you have had a problem with a customer? What did you do? What did you learn from that experience? What would you do differently?

- Describe a situation where you had to deal with a particularly angry customer? Why were they upset? How did you calm the customer down? What would you do differently?

- What steps do you take to find out whether customers are satisfied with the service you are offering?

Figure 5.5 Example of evidence-based questions used when recruiting service providers

PERSONAL OBJECTIVES

'What gets measured gets done' is an old adage. How many individuals in your organisation have been set personal objectives that focus on customer service? This is a proven way of ensuring that everyone throughout the organisation works towards the customer. Objectives need to be set in a cascade fashion so that there is a link between what the organisation needs to achieve in terms of customer service, what the department has to achieve and individual objectives.

Personal objectives centred around the customer can focus on 'what' needs to be achieved, for example, 'Increase customer satisfaction scores from 8.8 to 9 out of 10 by quarter 3 this year as measured by the quarterly customer survey'. They can also set out the 'how', in other words the behaviours that need to be demonstrated and the steps that need to be taken, as shown in Figure 5.6.

Objective

Increase customer satisfaction scores from 8.8 to 9 out of 10 by quarter 3 this year as measured by the quarterly customer survey.

Steps to achieve

- Undertake root-cause analysis of customer issues and complaints.
- Hold 'Dealing with difficult situations' workshop with all members of staff.
- Provide one-to-one coaching following the workshop.
- Monitor issues and complaints levels and take corrective action.

Figure 5.6   Customer service objective and steps to achieve it

The 'how' of a personal objective often links to an organisation's competency framework or behaviours. By measuring how people perform as well as what they achieve, a more rounded view can be obtained. It is also possible to assess development needs of the individual and link these to the competency framework. This can be achieved by reviewing competencies at the same time as objectives.

Another approach which is growing in popularity is to use the balanced score card (Figure 5.7), developed by Kaplan and Norton in the 1990s as a means of objective setting and performance management. The benefits of the balanced score card are that it provides a

Financial	**Customers**
Creating shareholder value	*Meeting customer expectations*
Learning and growth	**Internal processes**
Driving advances to achieve results	*Bringing about improvements to achieve results*

Figure 5.7   Balanced scorecard

holistic view of performance. It is a useful means of linking individual objectives to business goals.

The balanced scorecard is favoured by many organisations as it provides a more rounded approach to factors that affect business performance, rather than focusing purely on financial results. Objectives can be set in the four areas of the balanced scorecard at organisational, departmental and individual levels.

Instead of focusing on past financial performance, the balanced score card ensures that individuals are set objectives in the areas of customer, learning and growth and internal processes. Thus it encourages objectives to be set in four areas that are critical to organisational success.

Barking and Dagenham Council used the balanced scorecard as a performance management system for the Council. They adapted its emphasis to focus more on the community and used the framework as a vehicle for delivering the Council's vision.

For more information see *The balanced scorecard: translating strategy into action* by Robert S. Kaplan, David P. Norton (Harvard Business School Press, September 1996, ISBN: 0875846513).

PERFORMANCE MANAGEMENT CYCLE

However objectives are set, be it linked to values and competencies, customer service per se or the balanced scorecard, it is vital that the manager monitor and measure performance on an on-going basis and give regular feedback so that there are no surprises. Many organisations with whom I work now undertake performance reviews once every two to three months rather than waiting for the annual or biannual appraisal. In this way they are able to hold short one-to-one meetings that provide both motivational and developmental feedback on an on-going basis. The performance management cycle illustrated in Figure 5.8 starts with a two-way discussion around the setting of 'SMART' (specific, measurable, achievable, realistic and time-bound) objectives. At the same time a discussion needs to take place to clarify

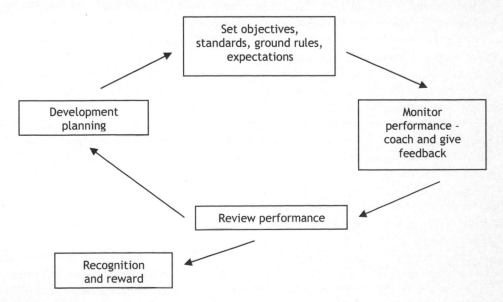

Figure 5.8   Performance management cycle

expectations around the areas of standards expected as well as ground rules for working together. The manager needs to monitor performance on an on-going basis and give regular feedback. It is also helpful to provide coaching support to boost an individual's confidence and develop competence. Formal reviews of performance can result in reward and recognition of exceptional performance and a plan of action to address development areas.

MEASURING CUSTOMER ORIENTATION THROUGH 180° AND 360° FEEDBACK

One method for measuring individual customer orientation is the use of 180° and 360° feedback. 360° feedback is direct feedback on how an individual is performing from all the people with whom he or she deals (see Figure 5.9).

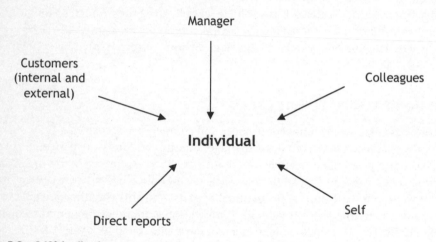

Figure 5.9   360° feedback

180° feedback normally involves people who do not have direct reports receiving feedback from their managers, colleagues and customers.

Collecting views from a wide range of people with whom the individual interacts is a useful means of assessing their relationship. It also gives a fuller picture than the downward feedback (boss to subordinate) that happens during appraisal. Many organisations now offer 360° feedback to the management population and 360° or 180° feedback to members of staff so that they each receive a rounded view of their performance.

360° feedback helps individuals identify their strengths and areas for development. Individuals may already be aware of some of this feedback, but some may highlight what had been blind spots for individuals. They may not have been aware of the impact of their behaviour on others.

Agencies such as Shine (www.shinefeedback.biz) can help design and administer a 360° questionnaire. Using an external agency helps ensure confidentiality; people are often more open in their comments if they know that these will not be directly attributed to them and the feedback will be collated independently.

If you decide to develop and administer 360° feedback yourself, it is helpful to devise a questionnaire that allows individuals to score as well as provide comments to support their scores. This can be paper-based or online. Often it is helpful to hold orientation sessions with those people who will take part in the feedback – including the individuals themselves as

---

Rate the individual on a scale of 1 to 6, where:

1 = totally uncharacteristic, does this up to 10% of the time
2 = not characteristic, does this 30% of the time
3 = not very characteristic, does this 50% of the time
4 = somewhat characteristic, does this 70% of the time
5 = characteristic, does this 90% of the time
6 = totally characteristic, does this 100% of the time

Your rating

Constantly drives for higher standards of customer service.   _____

Seeks feedback from customers.   _____

• What behaviours does your manager display that help you to do your job?
  _____

• What behaviours does your manager display that are not helpful for you to do your job?
  _____

• What should the individual be doing that they are not doing now?
  _____

Figure 5.10   Example of a 360° questionnaire

they will also need to self-assess their behaviour. The orientation will allow you to explain the purpose of the feedback, and how it will be used as well as questions of confidentiality and how to complete the questionnaire. Figure 5.10 shows an example of part of a typical 360° feedback report.

The process for undertaking 360° feedback is generally:

• Design a questionnaire.
• Trial this with several people to ensure that it is clear.
• Select participants who will give feedback. Explain the purpose of the feedback and gain their agreement to do this.
• Individual completes questionnaire.
• Issue questionnaire to participants stating timescales for response.
• Questionnaires returned for collation to independent body.
• Report produced and discussion of results held (this discussion is normally held between a representative of human resources or the external agency and the individual).
• Individual develops action plan as a result of feedback.
• Discussion held with manager about action plan.
• Individual communicates resulting actions to those who have taken part in 360° feedback.

TIPS ON GIVING FEEDBACK

As part of the orientation process, it is helpful to remind participants about the purpose of giving the feedback. Remind them to give balanced feedback across strengths and areas for improvement. People giving feedback should also base this on evidence not subjection, for example they could mention a specific behaviour and its impact on people and the task.

TIPS ON RECEIVING FEEDBACK

Recipients of 360° feedback need to remember that the feedback is about past behaviour. They need to listen and ask questions if they do not understand, rather than becoming defensive. At times they may need to ask for additional feedback from other sources to clarify or corroborate what has been said.

Corporately, 360° feedback helps to bring about an open organisational culture in which people can talk about issues that prevent the delivery of excellent service and take action to address these.

Measuring departmental service quality

It is also possible to measure customer service on a functional basis. This can be a one-off initiative driven by one department or function or it can be a company-wide programme to improve service delivery. The next section looks at both qualitative and quantitative methods of measuring internal service delivery at a departmental or team level.

Most departments or teams can set objectives or key performance indicators relating to customer service that can be measured. These can focus on performance relating to both internal as well as external customer needs. Having departmental customer service objectives gives everyone a focus. It is then essential that members of the team or department are actively involved in seeking feedback from customers on their performance against these measures. This will ensure a greater degree of ownership and responsibility for subsequent actions.

The first step is for each department to identify who are their key internal customers, that is, the people to whom they give a service. The list can be wide ranging. Here is an example of the internal customers of the finance department of one retail organisation:

- chief executive
- board of directors
- retail operations director
- retail operations managers
- unit managers
- treasury
- all other head office departments.

As described in Chapter 2, like any other form of research it is important to segment the target audience so that the opinions of each discrete customer type are canvassed. For example, the board of directors has different needs and expectations of the service delivered by the finance function than do the unit managers.

START WITH QUALITATIVE RESEARCH METHODS

As with external customer service measures, begin your measurement programme by gaining qualitative feedback first from internal customers. Internal customer focus groups and one-to-one interviews are typically a good place to start exploratory internal customer service research.

It is helpful to the department concerned to bring in an independent facilitator or interviewer to conduct the research. This helps reassure customers of the independence of the study and ensures a more open and honest discussion as well as overcoming bias.

Here is an example of the running order of an internal department's customer focus group:

1 Introductions and purpose of the focus group
2 Discussion on how often customers make contact with the department and the reasons why
3 What the department does that helps customers
4 What the department does that hinders customers
5 What the department should do differently in the future.

One other department used a very simple format:

• What is positive about the service this department provides?
• What can you rely upon this department for?
• What frustrations and concerns do you have in dealing with them?
• What aspects of their service would you like to see improved?

As with external customer focus groups, it is best to run internal groups with between eight and ten people. Make sure that the people attending are from a homogenous group. For example for Finance, separate groups were held with retail operations managers and unit managers as they had differing opinions.

In practice I find that more senior people in organisations are less likely to have the time or inclination to attend a focus group. Often one-to-one discussions are more fruitful. Here is an example of the running order of the one-to-one in-depth interviews held on behalf of a finance department. The order is sketched out only as this is an exploratory discussion and the conversation needs to be driven by the internal customer's agenda.

1 Introductions and purpose of the research
2 Confirm confidential nature of the discussion
3 Ask, in an ideal world, what is most important to the individual about the service they could receive from a Finance department (prompt and list attributes)
4 Hold discussion about what in their opinion, finance department do well (prompt where appropriate)
5 Hold discussion on what finance department could do better (prompt where appropriate)
6 Refer back to ideal list of service attributes, ask them to prioritise which attributes finance department should improve above all others
7 Thank the participants, explain what happens next and close discussion.

FOLLOW UP WITH QUANTITATIVE RESEARCH METHODS

Once the exploratory, qualitative research has taken place, the internal steering group is in a position to review the results and to decide whether further research is needed across a wider population. Often, in practice, I find that the quality of the information received from focus groups and one-to-one interviews is good. This provides the internal steering group with ample feedback to develop an improvement action plan.

If further information is needed, then questionnaires (postal or online) as well as telephone surveys are effective follow-up mechanisms.

Figure 5.11 shows an example of a simple questionnaire that one department sent to all its customers through the internet. It received a 45 per cent response rate.

Please help us to improve the service we give you by taking a few minutes to answer these questions.

On a scale of 1 to 10, where 1 = poor and 10 = excellent, rate the service we give you as follows:

	Your score
Ease of contact	_____
Helpfulness of staff	_____
Knowledge of staff	_____
Responsiveness to your requests	_____
How well we keep our promises	_____

Figure 5.11   Part of internal departmental online survey

Another department, which had set service standards in consultation with its customers, used the cards shown in Figure 5.12 with all its correspondence, by telephone, post or email, to gain feedback on how well it was meeting its service standards.

'Mystery shopping' is also an interesting way of gaining feedback on the quality of the service that internal departments provide. One organisation established a working party to create a set of service standards for all of the business's functions. These included standards for answering the telephone as well as email response.

The working party then set up a team to make calls and send emails to each of the departments. If the standards were met during the 'mystery shop' then the person answering the call or sending the email received an instant reward such as a bunch of flowers or box of chocolates.

If you are going to undertake internal service measurement, here are some things to watch out for:

1 Make sure that departments co-ordinate their measurement – otherwise people will be 'bombarded' with questionnaires and requests to attend focus groups all at the same time.
2 Do let internal customers know the results of the surveys – send them a copy of the results as well as letting them know your improvement action plan.
3 Do take action as a result of the surveys – one department I know took 12 months to review their customer feedback – as a consequence service levels had dropped further and internal customers were understandably sceptical that any action would be taken. This created a poor reputation for the department.

Just as when measuring external customer satisfaction, it is healthy not to rely on one measurement technique to monitor internal service quality.

One rental car company adopted the following forms of measurement across the year in all departments:

Telephone calls

Date of call...   Your branch/dept..

Name of branch/dept being commented upon; please be specific..

1.   Number of telephone rings before call was answered?

        0-3 ☐   4-6 ☐   7-9 ☐   10+ ☐

(If you answer 'no' to any of the following questions, please complete details in the comments section provided)

2.   Was the call answered correctly?   Yes ☐   No ☐

Branches – appropriate greeting and company name
Department Manager – name only
Other Staff – department and name

3.   Did the dept/branch provide the information requested without
        undue delay?   Yes ☐   No ☐

4.   If not, did the dept/branch take responsibility for the call?   Yes ☐   No ☐

5.   Was the call handled in a friendly/courteous/confident manner?   Yes ☐   No ☐

Additional comments:

Correspondence

Date ....   Your branch/dept ....

Name of branch/dept being commented upon ....

Form of correspondence   Memo ☐   Form ☐   Email ☐

1.   Was the completed document legible and well presented?   Yes ☐   No ☐

2.   If a response was required, was a reply by date given?   Yes ☐   No ☐   N/a ☐

3.   Was the form or document received the current issue
        (where applicable)?   Yes ☐   No ☐   N/a ☐

4.   Was the attachment referred to in correspondence attached?   Yes ☐   No ☐   N/a ☐

5.   Was adequate information provided in the correspondence?   Yes ☐   No ☐   N/a ☐

Additional comments:

Figure 5.12   Internal survey relating to service standards

1 Customer service visit: each department was visited by a director or senior member of the management team (not from their own area) who assessed the quality of the systems and procedures employed against given criteria.
2 Telephone, email or written correspondence mystery tests: the mystery shop programme measured service quality over a range of communications methods.
3 Internal comment card: customer comment cards were sent out to all customers who contacted departments whether by phone or email or in writing.
4 Internal customer questionnaire: all departments were assessed by their internal customers through the completion of a detailed quarterly questionnaire.
5 Internal customer focus groups: customer focus groups were run throughout the year.

Measuring organisational service quality

If you are beginning a culture change programme, a useful first step is to measure internal service quality to assess where improvements need to be made. Many organisations also carry out annual surveys to assess the state of the business and where improvements need to be made. Healthcare organisation BUPA, for example, carry out an annual survey. The results can be broken down by department and by individual manager.

Looking at the elements of the service-profit chain that relate to internal service quality and employee satisfaction and retention, which I desccribed in Chapter 1, (see Figure 5.13) provides a good steer of the type of measures to put in place.

Internal service quality	*Employee satisfaction and retention*
Right tools for the job	Leaders who focus on the customer
Adequate resources	Leaders who promote excellent service
Effective and efficient systems	Clear direction setting (goals, service vision and customer promise)
Appropriate structure	Open communication
Appropriate job design	Appropriate employee selection and development
Relevant core competencies	Empowerment
Effective internal measures	Coaching
	Effective team building and management
	Reward and recognition

Figure 5.13   Internal service quality and employee satisfaction and retention

EMPLOYEE SURVEYS

Employee surveys are a useful gauge of employee morale. The response rate to employee surveys tells the business how open and honest their communication lines are. It is normal to expect around a 60 per cent response to this type of survey. One service organisation with whom I worked was disappointed to receive a 98 per cent response rate!

Normally every employee in an organisation is given the opportunity of completing this type of survey. Therefore the easier and clearer the survey is to complete, the better. It is worthwhile conducting exploratory research to ensure that the questions in the survey are appropriate and meaningful to individuals. This is usually done through one to one interviews and employee focus groups that can be held with representatives from across the organisation. If your organisation is unionised, it is helpful to gain agreement to the survey from the appropriate unions. Another tip is to set up a working party drawn from representatives across the business to review the exploratory research and give final sanction to the questions to be used.

As leadership is a key influencer in determining the customer orientation of individuals, do not shy away from including questions on management and leadership style as part of the survey.

A cautionary measure is to pilot the questionnaire amongst a small sample of the target population. This allows you to test for understanding and ease of completion.

To ensure that everyone receives the questionnaire, the survey can be sent to employees with their salary packet. Another approach is to send the survey to employees' private addresses. In either event, response rates will increase if dedicated, uninterrupted time is given to employees during work to complete the questionnaire.

Once the survey has taken place, it is best practice to make the results public. Many organisations use the outcomes to index employee satisfaction levels as well as other areas of importance to the business.

As well as publishing the results of the employee survey, it is essential that each department and manager, as well as the organisation as a whole, develops an action plan for addressing key areas of improvement (see Chapter 7).

EXAMPLES OF EMPLOYEE SURVEY

Figures 5.14 and 5.15 show two examples of an employee survey (taken from *Compendium of customer service questionnaires and inventories*, Sarah Cook, Gower Publishing, Aldershot, 2002).

CUSTOMER ORIENTATION SURVEYS

One of the disadvantages in using employee attitude surveys to measure service effectiveness is that they can cover a myriad of topics. An alternative quantitative method of assessing an organisation's orientation towards the customer is to undertake customer orientation culture surveys. Culture is the glue that binds the organisation together, the 'way we do things around here'. It is a helpful starting point to identify the culture in your organisation at the beginning of a customer service programme and to continue to do this on a regular basis. In practice large and geographically spread businesses have many different types of cultures. Figure 5.16 shows an example of a culture audit around customer orientation (taken from

	Agree strongly	Agree	Disagree	Disagree strongly
1. I understand the aims and objectives of the organisation.	1	2	3	4
2. My work environment (e.g., lighting, heating, layout) is good.	1	2	3	4
3. I have access to the tools I need to do my job well (e.g., printer, fax, computer).	1	2	3	4
4. I feel proud to be working for the company.	1	2	3	4
5. My salary adequately reflects the market rate for the quality and quantity of work that I do.	1	2	3	4
6. I am given appropriate recognition for the work that I do.	1	2	3	4
7. I receive good quality training to help me perform my job well.	1	2	3	4
8. I receive sufficient quality training to help me perform my job well.	1	2	3	4
9. I receive good quality training to aid my future development.	1	2	3	4
10. I have a clearly defined career development path.	1	2	3	4
11. I have a high degree of confidence in senior management.	1	2	3	4
12. I believe that the management team keeps me well informed of company performance.	1	2	3	4
13. I am satisfied with the frequency of communication on company performance.	1	2	3	4
14. I am satisfied with the methods used for communicating company performance.	1	2	3	4
15. There is ample opportunity to feedback my opinions to senior management.	1	2	3	4
16. I feel that I am part of a team.	1	2	3	4
17. The objectives of my team are clear.	1	2	3	4
18. My role and responsibilities and those of my team are clear.	1	2	3	4
19. The workload in my team is evenly distributed.	1	2	3	4

Employee attitude survey

Help us to improve our working life.

Please indicate your degree of agreement or disagreement in response to each of the following statements.

There are no right or wrong arguments. Please be honest!

The questionnaire is entirely confidential.

Figure 5.14   Example of employee attitude survey – *continued*

	Agree strongly	Agree	Disagree	Disagree strongly
20. There are good working relationships between my immediate team members.	1	2	3	4
21. I have good working relationships with other teams.	1	2	3	4
22. I understand the role and responsibilities of other teams.	1	2	3	4
23. My immediate manager gives me help and support to do my job well.	1	2	3	4
24. I am involved by my manager in the decision-making process.	1	2	3	4
25. I am able to express my ideas and honest opinions to my manager.	1	2	3	4
26. I am set meaningful objectives by my manager.	1	2	3	4
27. I often get the opportunity to use my initiative.	1	2	3	4
28. I have regular review meetings with my manager.	1	2	3	4
29. My manager listens to and acts on my ideas.	1	2	3	4
30. My manager trusts and supports my decisions.	1	2	3	4
31. I enjoy working for the organisation.	1	2	3	4
32. The organisation has changed positively in the past 12 months.	1	2	3	4

33. What do you see as the positive elements of working in the organisation?

34. What do you see as the major areas you would like to see changed?

Please indicate the department in which you work:

Thank you very much for your comments.

Please return this form to:
by:

The results of the survey will be published by:

Figure 5.14   *concluded*

Employee satisfaction survey

Please answer the following questions as honestly as possible using the following scale:

Agree strongly	AS
Agree	A
Neither agree or disagree	NA
Disagree	D
Disagree strongly	DS

Your responses will be treated in confidence. No one will be identified as part of the results of this survey.

		AS	A	NA	D	DS
1.	I have received adequate training to prepare me to do my job well.					
2.	My work performance is evaluated fairly.					
3.	I am kept informed about decisions affecting my job.					
4.	Senior managers care about the wellbeing of employees.					
5.	My boss gives me appropriate recognition.					
6.	I am involved in decision making.					
7.	There are adequate opportunities for personal development.					
8.	I am paid fairly for the work I do.					
9.	I am happy with the working environment.					
10.	There is equality of opportunity.					
11.	The compensation and benefits the company offers are as good as other companies.					
12.	The compensation and benefits the company offers are better than other companies.					
13.	I am satisfied with the level of job security.					
14.	Morale is high.					
15.	I can say what I think without fear of reprisals.					
16.	I have sufficient work to do.					
17.	I have too much work to do.					
18.	Co-operation between departments is good.					
19.	I receive feedback from customers.					
20.	I believe what senior managers tell me.					
21.	There are adequate job opportunities for people with the appropriate skills.					
22.	Job vacancies are communicated fairly.					

Figure 5.15   Example of employee satisfaction survey – *continued*

	AS	A	NA	D	DS
23. There is sufficient contact between management and staff.					
24. My opinions are valued.					
25. I know what the organisation is trying to achieve.					
26. I know what is valued and important in the company.					
27. My performance is reviewed at least once every six months.					
28. I have ready access to the technology I need to do my job.					
29. The organisation makes sufficient use of technology.					
30. There is adequate opportunity to develop my career.					
31. There is no duplication of effort.					
32. I work in a safe environment.					
33. My boss jointly sets objectives with me.					
34. My boss provides me with regular feedback.					
35. My boss encourages my development.					
36. My boss delegates tasks appropriately.					
37. My boss encourages teamwork.					
38. My boss deals with conflict effectively.					
39. My boss manages change effectively.					
40. My boss is a good communicator.					
41. I am well managed.					
42. I understand what departments in other parts of the company do.					
43. I am proud to work for the company.					
44. I speak highly of the company to friends.					
45. The company has changed for the better in the past 12 months.					
46. The company has changed for the worst in the past 12 months.					
47. I am treated fairly by the company.					
48. I am treated with respect by my colleagues.					
49. Pay is matched to performance.					
50. This survey is a good thing to do.					
51. Managers will listen and act on the results of this survey.					
52. The results of this survey will be communicated to all staff.					

Please complete as appropriate:

- The one thing above all others that needs to **start** happening to make me more satisfied at work is:

Figure 5.15   *continued*

- • The one thing above all others that needs to **continue** to happen to make me more satisfied at work is:

- • The one thing above all others that needs to **stop** happening to make me more satisfied at work is:

Department name : _____

Thank you for your help. Your responses will be treated in confidence. No one will be identified as part of the results of this survey.

Figure 5.15   *concluded*

Compendium of customer service questionnaires and inventories, Sarah Cook, Gower Publishing, Aldershot, 2002).

CARD SORT

As an alternative to questionnaire-based customer orientation surveys, card sort is a technique that allows individuals to identify what is currently valued by the organisation and what should be valued in the future. The exercise is in two parts. In part one people representing different parts (or the same part) of the organisation are given a series of cards that they are asked to sort into piles, according to what is currently happening in the organisation:

- • What is currently valued a lot in the organisation.
- • What is valued to some extent.
- • What is not valued.
- • What is not valued at all.

Assess your organisation's customer orientation

Circle the degree of your agreement in response to each statement.

	Agree strongly 1	Agree 2	Disagree 3	Disagree Strongly 4
The most important aspect of our business is satisfying customers	1	2	3	4
Everybody has a customer – be it inside the organisation or outside	1	2	3	4
We have 'heroes' who champion the customer	1	2	3	4
Our organisation is not bureaucratic	1	2	3	4
Customers say we're special	1	2	3	4
The majority of people provide a high quality of service	1	2	3	4
Customer service is a key corporate objective	1	2	3	4
You've got to talk the language of the customer to fit in round here	1	2	3	4
We recruit people whose attitude is orientated towards the customer	1	2	3	4
People work together as a team to serve the customer	1	2	3	4
Most of the stories which circulate seem to feature customers	1	2	3	4
Customer care is evident at Head Office as well as at the front-line	1	2	3	4
Our leaders demonstrate their enthusiasm for the customer	1	2	3	4
We are constantly finding new ways to satisfy our customers	1	2	3	4
We reward people for going out of their way for the customer	1	2	3	4
We encourage our customers to tell us if things are not right	1	2	3	4
We're always taking steps to implement new ideas to help the customer	1	2	3	4
Our systems and processes work smoothly	1	2	3	4
My manager sets a positive example in serving the customer	1	2	3	4

Figure 5.16   Example of culture audit – *continued*

	Agree strongly 1	Agree 2	Disagree 3	Disagree Strongly 4
We talk about the customer in largely positive terms	1	2	3	4
I have been given training in knowledge, attitudes and skills which help me to satisfy the customer	1	2	3	4
My personal objectives revolve around customer satisfaction	1	2	3	4
We have a clear understanding of the needs of our customers	1	2	3	4
Everyone is encouraged to ask for and act on feedback from customers	1	2	3	4
I refer to my customers by name	1	2	3	4
The focus of our business is on retaining existing customers as well as attracting new ones	1	2	3	4
Staff induction includes the importance of customer service	1	2	3	4
Senior managers spend time with customers	1	2	3	4
I am empowered to take decisions to help the customer	1	2	3	4
When a customer comes to me with a problem I take ownership of this through to resolution	1	2	3	4

Now add up your scores. Total: _____

The statements included in the questionnaire have been developed from research about what makes excellent customer-focused organisations.

Best practice customer-focused organisations:

- Demonstrate commitment to the customer from senior management down.
- Employ managers whose behaviours set a positive example of customer care.
- Actively listen to their customers and act on their feedback.
- Recruit customer orientated individuals and provide induction to them in customer service.
- Train and develop their people in customer-orientated attitudes, skills and knowledge.
- Empower their employees.
- Encourage problem ownership.
- Constantly measure customer satisfaction.
- Recognise and reward excellent service.
- Encourage continuous improvement.
- Focus on customer retention as well as attracting new customers.

Figure 5.16   *continued*

How to interpret your score

Score 60 or under:	Your organisation is customer-focused. Compare your scores with others. Study the areas in the survey where you score strong agreement. Discuss those areas where you have indicated there are blockages to providing excellent customer service.
Score 61 or over:	Your organisation can do much more to provide excellent customer service. Note the areas where you have scored poorly. Compare your scores with other people in your organisation. Agree a plan of action to address barriers to becoming a customer-focused organisation.

Figure 5.16   *concluded*

'Valued' means what is considered important, what is actively encouraged in behaviour, not just in words.

In part two, participants focus on the future and sort the same cards into four piles as follows:

- What should be valued a lot in the future in the organisation
- What should be valued to some extent
- What should not be valued
- What should not be valued at all.

Here is an example of some of the words that can be put on cards and used as part of this method:

1) Focusing strongly on the needs of the customer.	2) Planning for the long term.	3) Sharing knowledge.
4) Encouraging team work.	5) Working with different divisions to achieve the organisation's aims.	6) Being efficient.
7) Involving others in decision making.	8) Developing new products and services.	9) Continually striving for improvement.
10) Providing clarity on where we are going and what we want to achieve.	11) Rewarding performance that exceeds expectations.	12) Minimising error.

A card sort can be used as a discussion point as part of focus groups. Focus group participants work in groups of twos and threes to sort the cards. After the first sort as well as after the second each group discusses how they have sorted the cards and the reasons why. The differences between the first and second sort highlight areas for desired change for the future.

The information obtained from this method allows you to build a picture of the current culture of the organisation as well as what employees would like to see improved in the future.

RICH PICTURES

A qualitative and more creative method for investigating current and desired culture is to invite a cross-section of employees to depict how they see the organisation or their department currently and how they would like to see it in the future. Again comparisons can be made about the current and desired state and in-depth discussions held about what the pictures mean.

This method involves asking individuals to draw (or if they cannot draw to write words) to depict the organisation as if it was a building or as if it was a mode of transport (for example boat, plane, car, train). They are asked to show the environment in which the building sits or the mode of transport is travelling and other things that are around it.

By using expressive techniques such as this, people are able to visualise and vocalise current and desired states. Both card sort and rich pictures are qualitatitive methods involving views and opinions. The information gained from these techniques can then be substantiated using quantitative surveys to gain a measure of overall organisational customer orientation.

Assess your current approach to measuring internal service quality

Look at the following statements and assess your organisation:

Customer service measurement criteria	In place	Not applicable	Needs to be acted on or addressed
Our organisation has customer service measures in place at an individual, departmental and organisational level.			
Customer service is a key competency area for everyone in the organisation.			
Customer service is one of our organisation's values.			
Customer orientation is a key criterion in recruitment.			

Customer service measurement criteria	In place	Not applicable	Needs to be acted on or addressed
An individual's personal objectives include customer service.			
Our organisation uses the balanced score card approach to objective setting.			
One-to-one reviews of performance take place at least twice a year.			
Our organisation uses 360° feedback to measure performance.			
Each department in our organisation is aware of who their customers are.			
Departments have held internal customer focus groups and one-to-one interviews to establish customer needs.			
Departments use surveys to gauge the satisfaction levels of their internal customers.			
We have mystery-shopped the service provided to internal customers.			

Customer service measurement criteria	In place	Not applicable	Needs to be acted on or addressed
The department's objectives and key performance indicators are linked to customer service.			
We use a wide variety of measures to monitor internal service quality.			
We undertake an annual employee survey.			
We use methods to establish our current and desired culture.			
We have set objectives for customer service for the entire organisation.			

6 *Benchmarking*

Customers make decisions about an organisation's service quality based on their experience with a multitude of other service organisations. When measuring customer service, businesses need to take into account how they compare with other organisations in their own industry and other sectors. Benchmarking is a useful tool for making this analysis.

In this chapter we look at a variety of methods for measures which help provide an objective assessment of an organisation's customer service. We cover:

- What is benchmarking?
- How does benchmarking help measure customer service?
- Types of benchmarking
- The benchmarking process
- The European Foundation for Quality Management
- The Malcolm Baldrige National Quality Award
- Six Sigma
- Benchmarking organisations.

What is benchmarking?

Benchmarking is the process of comparing practices and procedures to identify outstanding performance and learn from this to bring about improvement.

Benchmarking was originally developed by companies operating in an industrial environment. In recent years, organisations such as government agencies, hospitals and universities have also discovered the value of benchmarking and are applying it to improve their processes and systems.

HOW DOES BENCHMARKING HELP MEASURE CUSTOMER SERVICE?

In a customer service environment no business can afford to be complacent. Customers' expectations are rising. Customers' experiences of service quality are not just formed by dealings with one industry or sector; what happens on the high street, online, at the bank, in a restaurant, on holiday, at the gym and many other customer 'touch points' influences people's expectations of service.

Products and services can now be easily replicated and sustained competitive advantage is becoming harder to attain. Customer service professionals need to take a wider perspective of what is happening in the marketplace rather than being restricted to their own area of expertise. By measuring your own, other parts of the organisation and different organisations' customer service practices and procedures, you can improve your own levels of service.

Benchmarking:

- Provides a greater awareness of the quality of service that your organisation provides;
- Allows individuals to see their service from a customer's perspective;
- Helps set performance goals;
- Brings about improvement in processes and practices;
- Increases efficiency;
- Enhances customer satisfaction.

TYPES OF BENCHMARKING

There are four main types of benchmarking that you can undertake to measure customer service:

1 internal
2 competitive
3 non-competitive
4 best in class.

Internal benchmarking

This involves making comparisons within your own business. There may be parts of your organisation that adopt similar processes or procedures with whom you can share information and make comparisons. For example, I worked with a financial service organisation that had three contact centres spread geographically across the country. Although they dealt with different types of customers and business, many of their processes and much of their structures were similar. It was therefore possible to benchmark the three different centres and to identify and apply best practice.

Competitive

This is where businesses measure competitor's service, for example by mystery shopping their business, or by questionnaires and surveys. It is normal to use an independent research agency to conduct this type of survey. They can then index your organisation against others. For example First Direct used an NOP survey to compare satisfaction with other banks. They found that 94 per cent of their customers thought that First Direct was better than other banks. They were also able to compare satisfaction ratings of their own customers with those of other banks.

Non-competitive

Here a business identifies other companies who, although they may not have the same customer base, deal with similar situations or adopt similar processes. Organisations can learn from them although they work in a non-competitive field. For example BAA, which administers seven British airports and some overseas airports, not only benchmarked its competitors but learnt from organisations that have to deal with crowd control such as Wembley Stadium and Ascot racecourse. The similarity was that these types of businesses need to move and feed thousands of people per day. There are several networking forums that allow customer service organisations to share ideas.

Best in class

There are certain organisations who over the years offer consistently high levels of customer service, such as Disney and department store Nordstrom in the US. These businesses are considered 'best in class'. They are used as a benchmark of best practice by other service organisations, who, although they may not be able to replicate exactly the style of service that the star organisations demonstrate, can still learn from them and be inspired to greater things. One organisation whose mission was to provide 'world-class service' was able to measure its service culture by making comparisons between itself and organisations such as telecommunications Orange and logistics company DHL.

The benchmarking process

Benchmarking should be a systematic and well thought-out process. If it is done properly it is not industrial tourism or measurement for measurement's sake.

There are six steps in the benchmarking process, shown in Figure 6.1.

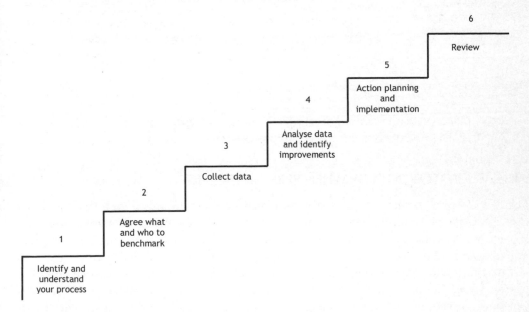

Figure 6.1   Six steps in the benchmarking process

Step 1 involves gaining in-depth knowledge of the processes or practices that you wish to benchmark. This involves mapping out exactly what happens when, who is involved and how long each step takes. Unless you have this type of information it is difficult to make direct comparisons.

Step 2 is agreeing what you want to benchmark and with whom. It is helpful to work with a project team to manage the project and the team will need to decide who you want to approach as benchmarking partners. At this stage too it is useful to decide how you will collect the comparative data, for example, face-to-face visits, observation, telephone surveys, questionnaires.

Step 3 involves collecting the data required to make comparison between your own and other organisations. Here it is important to agree the key metrics that you will use that can apply to all organisations taking part in the benchmarking study. Also, the benchmarking working party needs to be conscious of the differences that cultural influences may have in collecting data. The section below on 'What to watch out for when benchmarking' provides further guidance on how to address these issues.

Step 4 is analysing the data. It is important that this is in a format that allows you to make comparisons, as shown in Figure 6.2. In this way gaps in performance can be identified and improvement areas agreed.

Criteria	Your company	Company 1	Company 2	Company 3
Number of steps in the process	12	10	8	5
Number of people involved	7	6	4	3
Overall time taken	15 days	12 days	10 days	6 days

Figure 6.2   Benchmarking comparisons

Step 5 involves action planning and implementing the improvements.
Step 6 is reviewing the outcomes of the improvements.

WHAT TO WATCH OUT FOR WHEN BENCHMARKING

Just like any form of customer service measurement, do find a sponsor for a benchmarking exercise. Make sure you involve your team too in the design and implementation of the project. Set clear objectives for the benchmarking exercise and ensure that these are linked to organisational objectives. When starting a benchmarking campaign, do first conduct desk research to identify current best practice and sources of benchmarking partnerships. The website www.eCustomerServiceWorld.com is a useful starting point as is that of the National Customer Service Awards, www.customerserviceawards.com, which lists organisations that have won the annual events. See also the list of useful benchmarking contacts at the end of this chapter.

You can benchmark one-off customer service practices but studies show that you gain greater results by looking at customer service processes. Do not underestimate how much detail you need on your own processes and practices before you start to benchmark other people. Make sure that you map out your processes well. If you are not sure exactly how your process or practices work, it is difficult to make direct comparisons to other organisations. A process is a series of activities whose output benefits the customer. So for example, one service organisation identified the following key processes:

• recruiting new customers
• handling policy enquiries from existing customers

- handling claims from existing customers
- service recovery for existing customers.

Key processes can contain sub-processes. So the organisation in the example's service recovery process can be subdivided into further processes such as:

- pro-active service recovery
- goodwill
- handling rejected claims
- referrals to ombudsman.

I discuss process mapping in more detail in Chapter 7.

When contacting benchmarking partners, provide a brief description of the objective of the benchmarking study as well as who you are. In benchmarking, partnering means partnering, so both parties need to agree to share relevant information. Sometimes it is helpful to write out a simple agreement so that both parties know what to expect.

There are a number of organisations who can help facilitate introductions to benchmarking partners.

Be aware when measuring external organisations that their culture is probably different to your own. To gain real understanding of what lies beneath best practice, put in place key measures so that you can assess how different your benchmarking partner's culture is to your own. For example, measure some of the 'softer' elements in your own and partner organisation such as:

- recruitment process
- attrition rates
- training and development investment per employee
- leadership style
- communication
- performance management
- reward and recognition.

Once the benchmarking study has been completed, be prepared to take on board the findings, otherwise it becomes a useless exercise.

Benchmarking should not be considered a one-off exercise. To be effective, it must become an on-going, integral part of an improvement process with the goal of keeping abreast of ever-improving best practice in customer service.

Other models and approaches that help measure customer service

Benchmarking can be used in addition to qualitative and quantitative methods of measurement. One local borough undertook a period of public consultation which included a citizen's panel, customer focus groups and a MORI customer satisfaction survey.

At the same time it undertook a mystery shop assessment of its services to the public. It paid particular attention to internal customer satisfaction and ran an employee attitude survey to highlight what was going well and areas of concern.

It also benchmarked its services against Beacon Councils and the Pathfinder scheme for e-government as well as the National Performance Indicators published by Audit Commission reviews. The results of this phase, which lasted six months, became a springboard for developing a plan of action for improvements in customer service.

In the following pages, I provide an overview of different models and approaches that help organisations gain an objective view of their customer service effectiveness both in the private and public sector. They can be used as measures in addition to the customer-driven approaches we have described in Chapters 3, 4 and 5 and the benchmarking techniques outlined in this chapter.

EFQM EXCELLENCE MODEL

Another method of benchmarking your organisation's customer service is to adopt the EFQM Excellence Model as a measurement tool. The Excellence Model is a registered trademark of the European Foundation for Quality Management. The Excellence model adopts an holistic approach and uses an improvement framework based around nine key criteria. It is used to assess an organisation's performance.

The Excellence Model is best used when organisations wish to gain an objective measure of their business. Many organisations in the public sector are adopting this approach. The

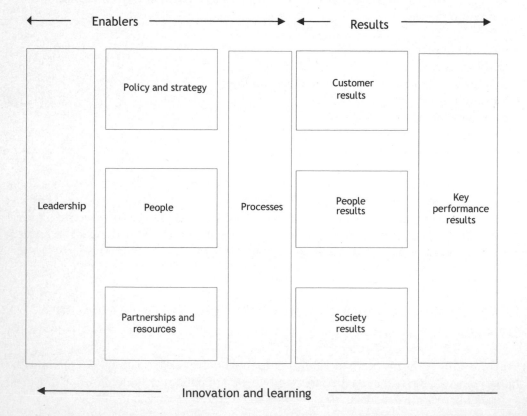

Figure 6.3   The EFQM Excellence Model

advantages of this method are that the assessment tool is comprehensive and encompasses employee as well as customer results. It also focuses on corporate social responsibility. The disadvantages of this method is that trained assessors need to apply the model.

South Tees Acute Hospitals NHS Trust started a number of pilot schemes for the implementation of the Excellence Model in 1995. They have seen a number of benefits from adopting this approach including midwifery-led care for pregnant women and low-dependency patients and more focused and better resourced high dependency and critical care.

At Accounts Office Cumbernaud, one of the 19 executive offices in the Inland Revenue, the use of the Excellence Model provided a comprehensive review of the organisation's activities and a robust benchmark against best-in-class.

In the model both enablers and results are assessed. The five key enablers of excellence are leadership; policy and strategy; people partnerships and resources; and processes. These enabling activities are the causal factors in achieving excellent performance – as demonstrated by people results, customer results and society results and then ultimately key performance results. Key performance results are the indicators of progress towards the organisation's aims and objectives, and are usually those reported in the organisation's annual report.

Enablers

LEADERSHIP

These criteria assess the leadership capability of the organisation. The following four criteria are covered:

- Leaders develop the mission, vision and values and are role models of a culture of excellence.
- Leaders are personally involved in ensuring that the organisation's management system is developed, implemented and continuously improved.
- Leaders are involved with customers, partners and representatives of society.
- Leaders motivate, support and recognise the organisation's people.

POLICY AND STRATEGY

This section measures how the organisation implements its mission and vision through the strategy and policies it adopts:

- Policy and strategy are based on the present and future needs and expectations of stakeholders.
- Policy and strategy are based on information from performance measurement, research. learning and creativity related activities.
- Policy and strategy are developed, reviewed and updated.
- Policy and strategy are deployed through a framework of key processes.
- Policy and strategy are communicated and implemented.

PEOPLE

How the organisation manages, develops and releases the knowledge and full potential of its people at an individual, team-based and organisation-wide level, and plans these activities in order to support its policy and strategy and the effective operation of its processes:

- People resources are planned, managed and improved.
- People's knowledge and competencies are identified, developed and sustained.
- People are involved and empowered.
- People and the organisation have a dialogue.
- People are rewarded, recognised and cared for.

PARTNERSHIPS AND RESOURCES

This section looks at how the organisation plans and manages its external partnerships and internal resources:

- External partnerships are managed.
- Finances are managed.
- Buildings, equipment and materials are managed.
- Technology is managed.
- Information and knowledge are managed.

PROCESSES

The criteria in this section look at process design and management:

- Processes are systematically designed and managed.
- Processes are improved, as needed, using innovation to fully satisfy and generate increasing value for customers and other stakeholders.
- Products and services are designed and developed based on customer needs and expectations.
- Products and services are produced, delivered and serviced.
- Customer relationships are managed and enhanced.

Results

In the assessment of results there are the following areas:

CUSTOMER RESULTS

What the organisation is achieving in relation to its external customers.

- Perception measures; these measures are of customers' perceptions of the organisation obtained through qualitative and quantitative research.
- Performance indicators; these measures are the internal ones used by the organisation to monitor, understand, predict and improve the performance of the organisation and to predict perceptions of its external customers.

PEOPLE RESULTS

What the organisation is achieving in relation to its people:

- Perception measures; these measures are of the people's perception of the organisation.
- Performance indicators; these measures are the internal ones used by the organisation to monitor, understand, predict and improve the performance of the organisation's people and to predict their perceptions.

SOCIETY RESULTS

These criteria relate to what the organisation is achieving in relation to local, national and international society:

- Perception measures; these measures are of the society's perception of the organisation.
- Performance indicators; these measures are the internal ones used by the organisation to monitor, understand, predict and improve the performance of the organisation and to predict perceptions of society.

KEY PERFORMANCE RESULTS

These criteria relate to what the organisation is achieving in relation to its planned performance:

- Key performance outcomes;
  - financial outcomes;
  - non-financial outcomes.
- Key performance indicators.

The EFQM Excellence Model is a proven measurement method which brings about improvement. The European Foundation For Quality Management also hosts awards. They can be contacted on www.efqm.org.

MALCOLM BALDRIGE NATIONAL QUALITY AWARD (US)

A benchmarking measurement that some Europeans who have American parent companies apply is the Malcolm Baldrige National Quality Award. This is an annual award made in the US to recognise companies for business excellence and quality achievement. The award intends to promote excellence and quality as well as sharing.

The seven criteria used for judging the award are based on:

1 senior executive leadership
2 information and analysis
3 strategic quality planning
4 human resource development and management
5 management of process quality
6 quality and operational results
7 customer focus and satisfaction.

More information on these measurement criteria can be obtained from www.quality.nist.gov.

SIX SIGMA

A measure of efficiency and effectiveness that many service organisations are beginning to adopt is 'Six Sigma'. This is a quality framework that has been implemented by many of the world's leading organisations. It aims to achieve error-free organisational performance and to improve efficiency by establishing quality principles and techniques.

Six Sigma drives better business results by gaining fundamental process knowledge using statistical frameworks. It has disciples in many businesses taking on the roles of green belts, black belts and master black belts. The popularity of the Six Sigma technique has grown out of the phenomenal results that General Electric in the US produced after adopting this methodology. In three years, General Electric added $2 billion to their bottom line.

Six Sigma is a thorough quality process program. The Six Sigma programme is unique to the requirements of the organisation and involves a five step improvement model known as 'DMAIC'.

Six Sigma is in fact a statistic. The Greek letter σ, sigma, describes a unit or value of efficiency in processes and procedures. It is used to describe variability or standard deviation in a set of figures. Six sigma quality is 99.99966 per cent. The higher the sigma rating the lower the number of defects. So if you make a widget and every one is perfect until the 294 117th widget, the quality level would be 99.99966 per cent (6 sigma). Ninety-nine percent efficiency, for example, equates to 3.8 sigma.

Originally started in manufacturing industries, Six Sigma is now being adopted by many service organisations. The benefits of the approach is that in addition to making processes and procedures more effective, Six Sigma focuses on what is important to customers. This is done by working with customers to identify the vital attributes that have the most impact on quality (often called critical to quality characteristics).

There are five steps in the Six Sigma improvement process, and these are shown in Figure 6.4.

Figure 6.4   The Six Sigma improvement process

1 Define critical quality characteristics: this helps identify and prioritise areas for improvement.
2 Measure current performance of these attributes. This involves putting reliable metrics in place.
3 Analyse the results to help identify the gap between the current and desired performance.
4 Improve: make data-driven improvements to processes and procedures by being creative and finding better ways of doing things.
5 Control the improvement areas to ensure that retained gains are maintained.

Six Sigma is a useful measurement tool for those organisations who wish to improve the efficiency and effectiveness of their customer processes. Six Sigma methodology has many advantages in that it is thorough and rigorous. Its downside is that it focuses on process improvement and does not take into account many of the cultural issues involved in delivering excellent service.

ISO 9000

Another external measure of customer service is ISO 9000. This is a quality system designed to help businesses ensure that their processes meet customer needs. Organisations that achieve ISO 9000 accreditation report benefits as:

- becoming more efficient;
- achieving customer satisfaction;
- reducing costs.

The methodology focuses on continually developing, documenting, implementing, monitoring and improving processes.

There are four phases to applying ISO 9000, as shown in Figure 6.5.

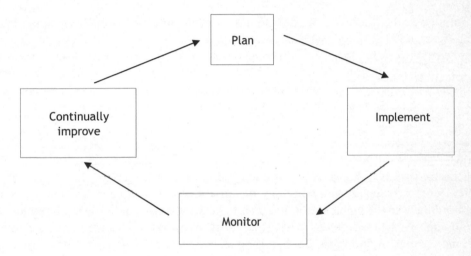

Figure 6.5   Applying ISO 9000

To develop a quality management system an organisation must plan strategically to set objectives that meet customer needs. This means first identifying the needs of the customer and key stakeholders and documenting what the quality management system requires.

Having established needs, a thorough assessment should take place by an external organisation to identify the organisation's current performance against desired performance and any gaps between the two. This provides the company with information on what processes need to be created or improved to meet customer needs.

Improvement actions are then put in place to close the gaps. If the quality management system is in conformance with ISO 9001:2000, the organisation may at this time decide to seek certification for this or to apply for a national quality award. Accreditation and registration are achieved after an external body audits the organisation to ensure that it conforms to the requirements of ISO 9001:2000.

Once an organisation is successfully certified, it needs to continually monitor its performance. The organisation will continue to be visited at regular intervals each year to ensure that the standard is maintained.

The final and on-going phase is for organisations to continue to improve their quality management system for the benefit of the customer.

Organisations who apply and measure themselves against ISO 9000 are often in the public sector. The advantages of this method is that it ensures that a quality system is in place. However, like Six Sigma, it focuses on processes and does not measure service orientation in terms of attitudes or behaviours.

Six Sigma is popular in both the private and public sector. In the public sector there are other initiatives that also prove useful measurement tools:

- Charter Mark
- Best value
- Beacon scheme
- Pathfinder.

One council in the south east of England has focused continually on the customer for the past 15 years. It has achieved ISO 9000 accreditation and has been awarded Charter marks for many of its services. It also has Beacon council status and was one of the all-service pilots for the Best Value programme. Using the Best Value model of 'challenge, compare, consult and compete', it incorporated the EFQM Excellence Model into this approach as a self-assessment tool. The result has been a continual and improving focus on the customer.

CHARTER MARK

The Charter Mark is a government award scheme open to organisations that deal directly or indirectly with the public and voluntary organisations that receive at least 10 per cent of their funding from the public sector. Its aim is to help organisations in the public sector focus on and improve their customer service. Since it began in 1992, the Charter Mark scheme has been successful in promoting and recognising service excellence. Award of the Charter Mark status means that organisations are delivering a first class service.

The end of 2003 has seen the introduction of six revised criteria for the Charter Mark, which will now become a 'customer service standard'.

To achieve the standard, organisations need to satisfy the following criteria:

Criterion 1: sets standards and performs well:

- sets clear service and performance standards by consulting customers;
- meets those standards;
- monitors and reviews performance against standards and publishes the results; and designs, puts into practice and monitors standards with as little unnecessary paperwork and administration as possible.

Criterion 2: actively engages with customers, partners and staff:

- actively works with (engages with) customers, partners and staff to make sure it delivers high-quality services;
- consults and involves present and potential customers of public services, partners and staff;

- is open, and communicates clearly and effectively in plain language and in a number of different ways; and
- provides full information about services, their cost and how well they perform.

Criterion 3: be fair and accessible to everyone and promote choice:

- makes services easily available to everyone who needs them, offering choice wherever possible; and
- treats everybody fairly in access to services and service delivery, and pays particular attention to people with special needs.

Criterion 4: continuously develop and improve:

- always looks for ways to improve services and facilities, particularly when using technology;
- puts things right quickly and effectively;
- learns from, and improves as a result of complaints, compliments and suggestions; and
- has a clear, well-publicised and easy-to-use complaints procedure, with the opportunity for independent review wherever possible.

Criterion 5: use resources effectively and imaginatively:

- financial management is effective; and
- resources are used effectively and imaginatively to provide best value for taxpayers and customers

Criterion 6: contribute to improving opportunity and quality of life in the communities served:

- has reviewed and is aware of its impact and potential usefulness in the local and national communities served; and
- has made some contribution to enriching the social or economic life of those communities, beyond the strict requirement of excellent service delivery, through positive, discretionary initiatives and imaginative use of resources.

There are sub-criteria in all six areas of the standard. A self assessment tool is available on www.chartermark.gov.uk.

The Charter Mark is a useful, objective measure of standards of customer service.

BEST VALUE

The best value scheme is a government initiative which aims to provide value for money services to the user in the public sector. In essence it is a performance management framework which was designed to act as a mechanism for driving continuous improvement. Part of the benefits of this scheme is the sharing of best practice to raise standards across the board.

Best value uses a process called the four Cs to bring about improvement: challenge, compare, compete, and consult. For more information contact www.idea.gov.uk/best value.

BEACON SCHEME

The Beacon scheme identifies excellence and innovation in the public sector. The scheme exists to share good practice so that organisations can learn from each other and deliver high quality services to all. It holds a series of learning exchanges, open days and other learning activities and is a useful source of benchmarking information.

Each year, the government selects themes for the beacon scheme chosen as they are vital to improving the quality of life in local communities.

Beacon status is granted to those organisations who can demonstrate a clear vision, excellent services and a willingness to innovate within a specific theme. However, to obtain beacon status, applicants must demonstrate that they have good overall performance, and not just in the service area for which Beacon status is awarded. See www.idea.gov.uk/beacons for more information.

PATHFINDER

Pathfinder is the name of an e-government initiative. Between June 2001 and June 2002, the Office of the Deputy Prime Minister funded 25 Local Government Online Pathfinder projects, with the aim of exploring and developing new ways of implementing e-government.

The pathfinder partnerships involved 110 local authorities and many public and private sector partners. They focused on a wide range of e-government issues designed to improve access to services and information, including exploration of new access channels such as digital TV, new ways of interacting with customers, such as smart cards and remote access centres, e-procurement, and the automation of back-office systems. More information on Pathfinder and e-government can be found on www.lgolpathfinder.gov.uk/.

Benchmarking organisations

Benchmarking organisations that are useful sources of information and contacts are as follows:

- Fit for the Future www.fitforthefuture.org.uk
  This is the UK's national best practice campaign led by the Confederation of British Industry. It aims to make the UK more productive and globally competitive. It encourages an open exchange of ideas and expertise and identifies sources of information and advice available to help companies make real change towards business excellence.
- Institute of Customer Service www.ics.com
- Customer Service Network www.customernet.com
- Institute of Quality Assurance www.iqa.org
- British Quality Foundation www.quality-foundation.co.uk
- Benchmarking in UK www.benchmarking.co.uk

PUBLICATIONS AND WEBSITES

- Customer Management (run by Quest Media, who also organise the Institute of Customer Service annual conference)

- CCF magazine (formerly Call Centre Focus)
- Customer First (magazine of the Institute of Customer Service)
- Customer Service News
- eCustomerServiceWorld www.eCustomerServiceWorld.com
- CRM-Forum www.crm-forum.com
- Customer Service Awards www.customerserviceawards.com

In addition the Audit Commission, an independent body responsible for ensuring that public money is used economically and effectively (www.audit-commission.gov.uk) is a useful source of data. It publishes National Performance Indicators for public sector bodies on an annual basis.

Assess your current approach to benchmarking

Look at the following statements and assess your organisation:

Customer service measurement criteria	In place	Not applicable	Needs to be acted on or addressed
Our organisation benchmarks customer service internally.			
Our organisation benchmarks the customer service of our competitors.			
Our organisation benchmarks non-competitively.			
Our organisation benchmarks for best in class.			
Our organisation uses EFQM as a measure.			
Our organisation uses Six Sigma as an improvement measure.			

Customer service measurement criteria	In place	Not applicable	Needs to be acted on or addressed
Our organisation has ISO 9000 accreditation.			
Our organisation has self-assessed against the Charter mark.			
Our organisation has shared information on Best Value.			
Our organisation has benchmarked against Beacon sites.			
Our organisation has benchmarked against Pathfinder businesses.			

7 *Analysing and Communicating the Results*

In this chapter I discuss how best to analyse and communicate the results of customer service measurement. In my experience the communication of the results of customer service measurement is as important as how you decide to gather feedback. Earlier we mentioned that 70 per cent of customer research does not get acted upon. The main reasons for this are that people do not analyse the data correctly or communicate its findings in a meaningful way.

In this chapter I cover:

- analysing qualitative and quantitative data
- presenting results
- reactions to feedback
- problem-solving techniques
- decision-making frameworks

Analysing customer service measurement results

As we have seen in earlier chapters, the methodologies that you use to measure both internal and external customer satisfaction need to be robust and sound. For example, if you have used a biased rating scale as part of a survey, the results will in turn be biased.

Throughout the data-gathering phase of customer service measurement, do keep in mind how you will analyse the data as well as to whom you will be presenting your results. One organisation I know of undertook 30 customer focus groups each lasting two hours. They had not considered how they would present the resulting data before they undertook the research. It took one person many weeks to sift through the results and draw worthwhile conclusions. One of the conclusions was that given the homogeneous nature of the target audience, a different research methodology would have been appropriate, for example hold six focus groups followed by a questionnaire to quantify the strength of feeling.

Here are some tips before you begin to analyse the information you have collected from customers:

- Keep the objectives for the measurement always in mind.

- Keep the analysis as simple as possible don't over-complicate things.

- Ensure that the data you have is fit for the purpose.

- Keep an open mind – unless the purpose of your research is to prove a particular theory, do not start the analysis thinking you already know the conclusions. This will cause bias in your analysis as you will probably subconsciously manipulate the findings to your prior conclusions.

- Ask someone else who has not been involved in the project to review your analysis before you present it to check that it is logical and that the findings make sense.

- Do not be afraid, where data is inconclusive, to instigate further research to clarify areas or probe further, particularly if important organisational decisions ride on the research.

QUALITATIVE DATA

The benefit of qualitative research such as one-to-one in-depth discussions and focus groups is that it allows the organisation to explore views, opinions and feelings. One of the downsides of this approach is that this information cannot often be easily quantified.

When analysing this type of feedback it is best to report back in narrative form. For example, here is the format of a report for one customer focus group meeting:

- background
- objectives
- who attended and when
- format and running order for the focus group
- findings under each topic area
- conclusions
- trends highlighted from this and other focus groups.

In the findings section for each of the topic areas under discussion, the facilitator lists all the points that have been raised. In the conclusions the facilitator summarises the key themes and issues arising from the research. If other focus groups have been run in a similar vein, they also highlight trends.

The benefit of qualitative feedback is the rich vein of emotion that the organisation can tap into. Be wary of losing the strength of feeling that focus groups and in-depth interviews provide. Include verbatim material from customers if this has been captured (tape and video are useful here).

QUANTITATIVE DATA

Questionnaires and other forms of survey provide data that can be analysed. The easiest form of analysis is to turn the data into percentages or mean scores. This allows comparisons to be made. When analysing:

- Use a spread sheet to enter data.

- Check that you are adding the correct data to arrive at percentages or means.

- To arrive at a mean score, multiple the number of respondents for each score, add the totals and divide this sum by the total number of respondents, for example:

Number of respondents	× Score	Total
23	1	23
25	2	50
38	3	114
45	4	180
44	5	220
70	6	420
66	7	462
45	8	360
20	9	180
12	10	120
Total 388		**Total 2129**

2129 divided by 388 = Mean score 4.87

Watch out when using mean scores alone however, as they can hide the range of responses – see Chapter 2.

- When presenting figures decide whether you wish to round scores between 0.51 to 0.99 up to the nearest whole number and round scores below 0.51 down or to present the figures to the nearest two decimal place, for example 3.59.

- Make sure that the questions and answers match.

- Note sample size – any sample under 100 lacks statistical validity; the greater the sample size the more valid the results. Make sure you put the sample size (n) on all the figures you present.

- Turn data into charts and diagrams. Information is easier to understand when it is visual, for example see Figure 7.1.

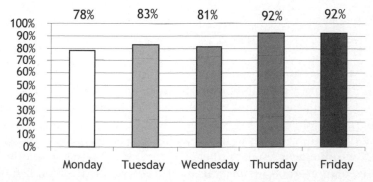

Figure 7.1   Percentage of calls answered within three rings by day of the week

- Make correlations between questions where appropriate, for example 81 per cent of respondents agreed that the service advisor was knowledgeable and 78 per cent agreed that the service advisor knew where to go for help.

- If your surveys have established importance ratings from customers as well as satisfaction, undertake a gap analysis to highlight where you are meeting customer expectations and areas for improvement.

- Where surveys have included open ended questions, analyse these too and present these as statistics, such as:

  Areas suggested for improvement ($n = 120$):
Improved speed of response to requests	46%
More knowledgeable staff	31%
More visits to customers	13%
Website more easy to navigate	8%
Other	2%

- Structure your findings so that they are logical and easy to follow. Here is an example of a report structure:

  Executive summary
  Background
  Objectives of survey
  Methodology
  Sample size
  Detailed findings
  Conclusions
  Recommendations.

Presenting results

When presenting the results of customer service measurement some advice is, think:

- Who?
- What?
- How?
- When?

Typically when preparing a presentation, we focus on what we need to say, rather than thinking 'Who is my audience?' Thinking about your audience and their needs helps you decide what information they need to hear. This in turn dictates how you present and when.

    The style of presentation needs to fit the audience. For example, I recently presented customer service measurement results to a board of directors. This was an information-giving session. The presentation was a summary using three PowerPoint slides. Before this I had facilitated a meeting with the sponsor and the project team, taking a day. Here, I presented the feedback and facilitated discussions on the conclusions, recommendations and action points the team wanted to come up with. This was very much an interactive, two-way process. The objective was to ensure that the project team members took ownership of the results and made a commitment to act on them.

Whether in a short presentation or a facilitated workshop, here are some tips when presenting results:

- Use diagrams and charts where possible – people interpret results more readily when they are presented visually. For example, Figure 7.2 is a histogram representing the length of time in which people have been members of a gym.

Class number	Number of years a member	Number of people
1	under 2	6
2	2.1 to 4	12
3	4.1 to 6	18
4	6.1 to 8	2
5	8.1 to 10	10
6	over 10	14

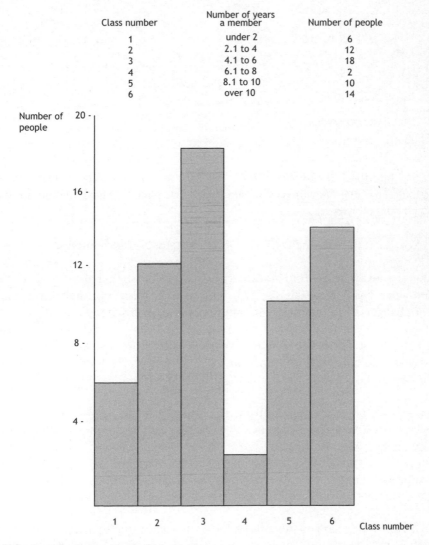

Figure 7.2   Length of gym membership in years

Figure 7.3 is a concentration diagram – a picture to show the location of events or problems. Remember the proverb, 'A picture is worth a thousand words.'

Delivery damage is marked on the diagram of the vehicle

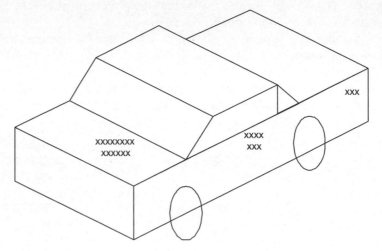

Figure 7.3   Damage to cars in delivery

- Use lots of white space for impact – make the presentation and report clear and easy to read. It is better to have a few images or paragraphs on a page, rather than clutter the report and make it difficult to read.

- Use colour to bring the data to life – it is more memorable and adds interest.

- Remember to convert figures into indexes wherever possible so that you can track feedback on an on-going basis. For example, providing overall satisfaction and loyalty indexes makes the changes in results easier to see and spot trends over time.

- If using PowerPoint, allow one slide to take 60–90 seconds on average to explain. Don't overload your audience with information. It is better to have fewer slides and greater discussion about the research, rather than 'death by PowerPoint'.

- Prepare a separate document summarising the results that can be given out at the end of the presentation. This stops people in the audience reading the presentation document whilst you are speaking.

- If your audience is very much into detail, provide the tabulations related to the research as a separate document so that they can look at the data after the presentation.

- Ensure where possible that you present results face to face so that there is an opportunity to ask questions and discuss outcomes. If appropriate, take one session to present the results and another to discuss reactions so that people have time to reflect. Develop a plan of action as a result of your presentation. This should include a plan on how other people will be informed about the results of the research and subsequent actions.

REACTIONS TO FEEDBACK

When presenting results, be aware that whether positive or negative, you will see a range of reactions to feedback at the presentation and probably afterwards:

Denial	Not ME! That's not true. That doesn't happen here.
Emotion	How dare they say that? How can they think that after all I've done for them?
Rationalisation	Ah, may be, BUT ... Well we've been so busy. The sample size was very small.
Acceptance	Well, yes, it's true. Yes, we could do better.
Change	I know what I am going to do. We can put this right by…

Denial is a very usual reaction to feedback. You may see people ignoring the results or assuming that the findings do not relate to them. In denial, people need evidence, facts to help them see that the findings are relevant.

You will probably see a range of emotions in people when they hear customer feedback – if it is positive feedback people can become embarrassed; if it is areas for improvement, people can become angry, tearful or withdrawn depending on their characters. In this phase it is helpful to give people time to reflect and see the feedback in perspective, before asking them to put together an improvement plan.

In rationalisation, people tend to justify away the feedback. Typically, people will pick holes in the research methodology or make excuses for their behaviour. To help people move through this stage, be future orientated, 'so given that we are so busy, what do we need to do differently next time?'

Once people accept the feedback, they need support and encouragement to bring about change.

You are likely to have a wide variety of reactions, therefore, to customer service measurement. It is useful to be aware of possible reactions and how to overcome them, prior to presenting the results. Do not 'massage' the results of the feedback however to overcome possible reactions. This might give you peace of mind in the short term but will mean that the voice of the customer is not heard.

Priorities for improvement

When presenting the results of customer service measurement, do make sure that you gain agreement to the key priorities for improvement. A gap analysis (see Figure 7.4) does help here.

Item	Importance score out of 10	Satisfaction score out of 10	Gap analysis
Speed of check in	6	6	–
Friendliness of staff	6	5	-1
Comfort of room	7	9	-2
Room service	6	6	–
Concierge service	8	10	-2
Bar service	9	8	+1
Restaurant service	8	8	–
Housekeeping service	7	9	-2

Figure 7.4   Gap analysis customer expectations versus satisfaction levels

There are also other tools that you can use to gain agreement to priorities, such as a four-box matrix or multiple voting.

Importantly, do not impose areas for improvement on the project team. They need to take ownership and responsibility for improvement areas. They are much likely to do this if they are instrumental in deciding priorities.

What sometimes happens, however, is that team members focus on improvement suggestions that they would like to see implemented. Be sure to challenge this, as the purpose of the customer research is to bring about improvements in service that the *customer* wants.

FOUR-BOX MATRIX

A four-box matrix is a simple way of prioritising customer and organisational needs. Two criteria are usually chosen to represent the x and y axes, for example 'Value to the customer' and 'Ease of implementation'. Each idea is rated according to these criteria; that is, is the ease of implementation high or low? Is the value to the customer high or low (as dictated by their importance ratings)? For example, one organisation's customers suggested the following ideas for improvement in the quality of service it provided:

- longer opening hours
- dedicated account manager
- quarterly reviews
- shortened monthly reports
- quicker response to email enquiries
- published standard response times
- newsletter.

In using the four-box matrix approach the priorities shown in Figure 7.5 were established.

To use the four-box matrix, take each of the improvement areas suggested by the research and plot them on the grid. All ideas plotted in the top right hand box would be the ideas this group would want to take forward first followed by the improvements in the bottom right hand box.

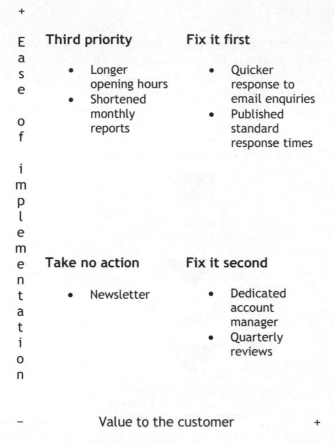

Figure 7.5   The four-box decision model

MULTIPLE VOTING

Multiple voting is a consensus-reaching technique that enables a group to select a proposal sufficiently acceptable for all members to support. It does not necessarily imply a unanimous vote, or a majority vote, but the result will be a proposal that no member opposes. It can be used:

• to narrow down a long list of options;
• to reach agreement on a course of action.

To use this technique, list all the available options. Allocate each participant ten points to 'spend' on their favoured proposals. If they strongly prefer one idea, they can spend all ten points on it, or they can share out the points, for example five, three and two; or four, three, two and one. Any combination which adds up to ten is acceptable.

Capture the results on a flip chart then lead a structured discussion on about five proposals that have received the highest scores. Continue these discussions until members of the team agree to dismiss all but one proposal.

Problem-solving tools

If working with a project team, before drawing up an improvement action plan, it is advisable to check that the team has identified the root cause of a customer issue. For example customers may be complaining that it is taking a long time for the phone to be answered. This may be a resource issue, a recruitment issue or a telephony issue.

There is a four stage process to problem solving in teams, as illustrated in Figure 7.6.

Define the problem
(Analyse potential causes)

Generate options
(Identify possible solutions)

Evaluate options
(Select best solution)

Implement solution
(Gain acceptance, develop action plan,
implement, review effectiveness)

Figure 7.6   Four stage process for problem solving

Setting up a problem solving team requires time and dedication. The ideal number of team members is between five and eight. The problem-solving team should be led by a co-ordinator who is trained in problem-solving techniques. It is essential that this is someone who recognises team dynamics, knows how to bring everyone into the debate and is able to deal with the inevitable conflict that can arise in such teams.

DEFINING THE PROBLEM

The first step in the problem-solving process involves defining what the problem is that needs to be addressed.

Cause and effect diagram

A cause and effect diagram breaks down a problem or an effect into its component parts. The causes of the problem are categorised so that the completed diagram looks like the skeleton of a fish (Figure 7.7). It can be used to:

* enable team members to use their personal knowledge to categorise the causes of the problem
* provide ideas for data collection and/or the root cause.

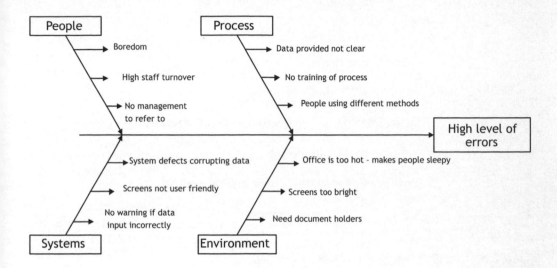

A high level of errors within the admin. team

People

Boredom

High staff turnover

No management to refer to

System defects corrupting data

Screens not user friendly

No warning if data input incorrectly

Systems

Process

Data provided not clear

No training of process

People using different methods

Office is too hot – makes people sleepy

Screens too bright

Need document holders

Environment

High level of errors

Figure 7.7   Example of cause and effect diagram

Remember, if you are using a cause and effect diagram, to ensure that you do collect data to substantiate possible causes of a problem, rather than stating opinions.

To draw a cause and effect diagram:

1 Write the problem or effect in a box on the right hand side of a flipchart. Draw a large arrow across the sheet, pointing to it.
2 Draw arrows indicating the main categories and pointing toward the central arrow at an angle. These are the causes of the problem.
3 In practice the main categories or causes are typically people, processes, systems and environment, but others may be used, such as customers and cost.
4 Brainstorm for specific details and attach each to an appropriate main category.
5 Break down the details further by brainstorming.
6 Gather and evaluate data on the possible causes.

In most cases, it's not of great importance where on the diagram you put a particular detail. Cause and effect diagrams are very useful when displayed publicly. You can invite people to add details, and you can show what progress is being made.

Cause and consequence diagram

The cause and consequence diagram (Figure 7.8) is another method for seeing the 'big picture' of a problem and establishing the causes as well as the consequences of a problem.

In the diagram, an improvement area is identified, for example 'lack of stock'. The consequences of this situation are then explored as well as all the possible causes.

Cause

Poor suppliers   Poor planning

No communication

Short lead times   Poor forecasting

Lack of stock

Poor morale   Customer dissatisfaction

Late deliveries

Loss of market share   Poor quality control

Consequence

Figure 7.8   Example of cause and consequence diagram

Both cause and effect and cause and consequence diagrams are useful in identifying all the causes of a problem. Therefore each cause can be addressed in the solution.

Problem checklist

A problem checklist is a less visual way of defining the problem. It consists of a series of questions that prompt and probe into the reasons for a problem. An example of this is:

- What is the problem?

- When does the problem occur?

- How does the problem occur?

- Why does the problem occur?

- Who does the problem affect?

- How often does it affect them?

- How does it affect them?

- Where does the problem originate?

- What is causing the problem?

- Who is causing the problem?

- What are the constraints in solving the problem (for example, time, money, resource)?

- When does the problem need to be resolved?

- What will happen if the problem is not resolved?

A problem checklist is a useful way of finding out the background to the problem. By talking through the questions, the project team has a far better understanding of the problem and is able to define the objectives for solving the problem, for example 'The objective is to define ways in which we can offer longer opening hours to satisfy customer demands.'

Pareto principle

During this phase of the problem-solving process be mindful of the Pareto principle. Pareto was an Italian economist who invented the 80/20 rule. Pareto analysis is a technique used to identify the 'vital few' from the 'many incidental' problem areas. It helps to determine which problems to solve and in what order.

To work out which problems to prioritise:

1 List the errors, costs or activities being analysed in order of magnitude, starting with the largest item.
2 Calculate the percentage of times each activity is mentioned as a cause.
3 Find the items which make up 80 per cent of the causes. Focus on solving these problems first.

GENERATING OPTIONS FOR IMPROVEMENT

Once the root cause of the improvement area has been identified, the project team can now generate options for solutions to the issue. This means opening up possibilities and being creative.

Edward de Bono describes creativity as 'the mental act of holding two unrelated ideas together simultaneously'. There is a lot of mystique around creativity, as if it is 'something that special people do'.

Typical blocks to being creative are all self-imposed. Mental dialogues take place such as:

- there's only one right answer
- that's not logical
- I must follow the rules
- that's not my area
- I don't want to be foolish
- I'm not creative.

It is useful to identify your own blocks to creativity. They may well include some on the above list. Generating options works only if you:

- keep an open mind
- entertain even those ideas that do not make sense
- suspend judgement

- have fun
- be prepared to try anything
- take a few risks.

Brainstorming

Brainstorming is a method of getting a large number of ideas from a group of people in a short space of time. It is the best-known and most frequently used technique for solving problems. It is particularly useful:

- when there is a need to collect a large number of possibilities or ideas;
- when looking for ideas for innovation;
- when looking for ideas to improve processes.

Here are a few principles of brainstorming:

- there should be no criticism;
- freewheeling is encouraged;
- quantity of ideas, not quality, is the first requirement;
- everything should be written down, however apparently impractical; you could use a flip chart and write all ideas on this;
- ideas should cross-fertilise from others;
- all ideas should be 'incubated' rather than rejected out of hand.

Alternatives to traditional brainstorming are:

Mind mapping

Take a piece of paper and write the topic area in a circle in the centre of the paper. Now let your ideas flow freely. Write your ideas on the paper. Join similar ideas by lines.

Post-it™ notes

Encourage individuals to write their ideas on Post-it™ notes. Use one Post-it™ per idea. After a suitable period ask everyone to put their Post-it™ on the table. Group these into clusters of ideas.

Round robin

Ask team members to write their ideas down privately on a piece of paper then go round the group in turn for a couple of times and ask for ideas before opening up for everyone to contribute. Write all ideas on a flip chart. Encourage people to build on others' suggestions.

Zaniest idea

Encourage weird and wacky 'off the wall' ideas. Anything goes! For example, what is the weirdest thing you could do with this product or service? What would you have to do not to promote this product? Then turn the weird idea into a more plausible one.

A – Z

Brainstorm possible solutions starting with A and ending with Z.

SELECTING AN OPTION

To select the best possible improvement option, the team may wish to use the four-box matrix or the multiple voting technique described earlier. Alternative techniques are paired choice matrix and criteria matrix.

Paired choice matrix

This method, illustrated in Figure 7.9, allows you to reduce a long list of possible solutions to the best one. To use the matrix begin with the first row (Solution A) and proceed across the row deciding which solution is the best solution between each pair. For example, you would first skip the choice between Solution A and Solution A, then choose between A and B, writing in the box your choice between the two. Continue across the row, making a choice between A and C, A and D, and so on.

	Solution A	Solution B	Solution C	Solution D	Score by row
Solution A	Employ new people	Train existing staff	Offer automated service	Extend opening hours	B, A, A
Solution B	Employ new people	Train existing staff	Offer automated service	Extend opening hours	B, B, B
Solution C	Employ new people	Train existing staff	Offer automated service	Extend opening hours	A, B, D
Solution D	Employ new people	Train existing staff	Offer automated service	Extend opening hours	A, B, D
Total times chosen	4	6	0	2	

Figure 7.9 Example of paired choice matrix for options to improve service

Repeat the process for each row until you have compared each possible pair. Then tally up the number of A's, B's, C's, and so on. The solution or solutions that you have chosen most frequently will become your short list.

Criteria matrix

A criteria matrix (see Figure 7.10) is a technique to choose the most suitable solution to a problem. It is useful for:

• ranking solutions in order of preference;
• selecting the best solution for the problem.

When developing a criteria matrix:

1 Decide on the criteria that are important for the solution, for example easy to implement, improves customer service, and so on. Probably two to four such criteria is the ideal. These criteria are written across the top of the solution matrix (see example).

Root cause	Possible solutions	Cost	Ease of implementation	Impact on problem	Acceptability to customer	Score C×E×I×A	Action?
Volume of telephone calls	Employ additional staff	1	3	5	5	75	No
	Rearrange team structure	5	4	2	2	80	No
	Train staff	2	3	1	2	12	No
	Introduce voicemail service	3	5	4	1	60	No
	Internet enquiry service	2	4	5	5	200	Yes

1 = low, 5 = high; action highest scoring solution first

Figure 7.10   Example of criteria matrix

2 Insert the root cause of the problem and possible solutions in columns 1 and 2.
3 Score the criteria for the solution, with 1 being low and 5 being high. (An alternative method is to score on a scale of 1 low to 3 high.)
4 Multiply the scores for each possible solution. That which scores the highest is most likely to be the best solution.

The result should be discussed, to ensure everyone agrees. If not, you may find that the criteria you used to score need to be amended. You may decide through discussion to give one or two criteria more weighting than others. In this case multiply the scores for the criterion that is most important by ten rather than five.

IMPLEMENTING SOLUTIONS

Once the group has agreed on one or more solutions, they are now in a position to implement an improvement action plan.

In considering how the solution will be implemented, a solution effect analysis is a technique for identifying the likely effects of a proposed solution to a project or problem. The diagram is similar in construction to the cause and effect diagram mentioned earlier.

A solution effect analysis is particularly useful in identifying potential benefits that may be gained from implementation of the solution as well as potential pitfalls.

A solution effect analysis (see Figure 7.11) is drawn by defining the solution under consideration and placing it in a box on the left hand side of the page. Then you need to identify the major categories where effects might occur. These are often customers, employees, costs, systems, environment and processes. The team brainstorms the possible effects that the solution might have and clusters them around the major categories. The effects can be both positive and negative. Once the effects of the solution have been determined, an assessment can be made as to whether the solution will be implemented effectively and what to do to minimise pitfalls.

A variation of solution effect analysis is force field analysis (see Figure 7.12). This is a technique which identifies the forces that help or obstruct change. It helps to assess the ease or difficulty in making a change and plan how to overcome barriers to a change. To produce a

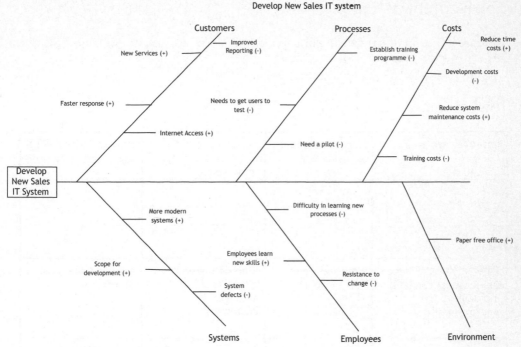

Figure 7.11   Example of solution effect analysis

force field analysis describe the change that is to be made. List the 'driving forces' on the left (these are the activities that will assist change). List the 'restraining forces' on the right (these are the activities that will obstruct change). For each of the forces, examine how easy it would be to change it and the impact of making the change. Reducing a restraining force is generally more effective than increasing a driving force.

← Driving forces	Restraining forces →
Training	Staff shortages
Customer satisfaction	Call routing
Process improvement	Additional tasks
Awareness	System performance
Procedures	System defects
Cost savings	Ignorance
	Unrealistic performance targets
	Boredom
	Commitment
	No time
	Uncontrolled changes

Figure 7.12   Example of force field analysis for introducing quality audits in a call centre

Improvement action planning

It is useful to record exactly what will happen, when and who is responsible as part of the improvement action plan.

Figure 7.13 shows an example of this format.

Name: _____

Improvement area	Target date for achievement	Action needed to achieve improvement	How and when will I take these actions?
Who amongst my team (colleagues) can help me achieve the improvement?	How and when will I involve them?	Who do I need to inform/consult amongst my customers?	How and when will I do this?

Figure 7.13   Example of customer care improvement action plan

START BACKWARDS

One alternative approach to action planning is to start backwards. Literally this means setting a goal and imagining that this has been achieved. Then working backwards from this point to identify all the steps that took place on the way. This is a brief description of the process:

- Decide what you want to achieve, your goal. Make this as specific as possible.
- Next, imagine that the goal has been achieved; what would be in place?
- Given that this is in place, what happened immediately before this to ensure this was in place?
- What happened before this?
- And before this?
- And before this?

Write down the responses to these questions. Now reverse the order of the responses so that the first response becomes the last. Put a time scale on each step and who will be responsible.

COMMUNICATING IMPROVEMENT ACTION PLANS

Communication is the life-blood of customer service measurement. Unless the results of measurement are communicated and also the actions that are going to take place as a result, measurement becomes a pointless exercise.

Think about who will be affected by the measurement and who needs to know or would like to know about the findings. (We find that people who are not directly involved in the service and may work in another part of the business are often interested in how customers perceive the company).

Best practice organisations develop a communications action plan specifically for customer service measurement, as shown in Figure 7.14.

To whom must we communicate?	What do we need to communicate?	How will we do this?	Who is responsible?	When will this happen?

Figure 7.14   Example of communications action plan

They use a variety of media, such as briefings, newsletters and web-sites, to communicate the results of the customer feedback and the resulting improvement action plan. Car hire company Avis, for example, has set up a website for customer service. Midlands Co-op include news of customer service in their main newsletter to 7000 employees. It also has a separate newsletter focusing on service excellence.

REVIEW

Improvement action plans and communication plans are important to prepare. The proof of the pudding, however, is whether anything happens as a result. It is the sponsor's responsibility to make sure that regular reviews take place of both improvement and communication plans. Making things happen as a result of customer service measurement is essential if your business wants to become and remain customer-centred. In the next chapter we look at ways in which feedback from customers can be used.

Assess your current approach to analysing and communicating results

Look at the following statements and assess your organisation where applicable:

Customer service measurement criteria	In place	Not applicable	Needs to be acted on or addressed
The analysis of our qualitative research includes customer responses verbatim.			
We undertake a gap analysis to identify priorities as part of our qualitative research.			
When presenting results, our presentation is focused on the needs of the audience.			
We anticipate the possible reactions to the research of those people to whom we are presenting.			
We identify priorities for improvement in a consultative manner.			
We use a problem-solving process to define problems, and to generate, evaluate and implement solutions.			

Customer service measurement criteria	In place	Not applicable	Needs to be acted on or addressed
Our organisation has a communications plan for disseminating customer feedback and resulting action.			
We regularly review the implementation of both our improvement and our communication plans.			

8 *Acting on Results*

In this chapter, I provide examples of how customer service measurement can help fashion an organisation's:

- vision, values and customer promise
- strategy
- structure
- leadership
- competencies
- training and development
- service standards and service level agreements
- process improvement
- reward and recognition strategy,

and how continuous measurement of customer service and on-going communication helps sustain a business's customer focus.

A holistic approach

In my experience, the result of listening to customers can help shape many aspects of the way an organisation is run. My observation is that often when companies receive the results of customer measurement, they 'tweak' one part of the business in response; for example, offering training in customer service or introducing service standards.

It is my belief that if an organisation is to be truly customer-focused on an on-going basis, it needs to adopt a holistic approach. Service excellence is like a wheel (Figure 8.1). At the heart are the vision and values of the organisation; the spokes round the edge represent different aspects of the business and its approach to customers. You can begin the wheel turning by taking hold of one of the spokes but if some of the spokes are stuck, the culture of an organisation will not change. The spokes all need to be turning freely and in the same direction.

Each of the elements representing the spokes needs to be turning to bring about culture change. Customer service measurement can provide the oil for the spokes.

Vision and values

Using customer research, it is possible to re-assess or create a vision for your organisation.

50/50 Conference facilitator, Peter Bishop, describes a vision as 'an image (not just an idea) of an attractive, compelling future state unique to an organisation that gives meaning to effort and motivates people to work together in the turmoil of a changing world'.

Figure 8.1   The service excellence wheel

A vision statement paints a picture of the desired future state, where the organisation wants to be. It is a statement of higher purpose.

The best vision statement are:

- short
- memorable
- meaningful
- motivational
- aspirational
- applicable to all parts of the organisation.

Disney's vision statement is 'to be the first in entertainment for people of all ages, everywhere'; 3M's is 'to solve unsolved problems innovatively'.

A mission statement (the word mission and vision often seem to be interchangeable) is a statement of strategic targets that enables the achievement of the vision. For example an organisation's vision statement might be 'creating a better community', while the mission statement accompanying this might be 'to offer learning and development opportunities to all'.

Working with the feedback from internal and external customers, I helped one organisation create a vision of its future state. This was fashioned by the board in consultation with key employee representatives. The board and I did this by referring to what was important to customers – both internally and externally and using their words to create a vision statement for the organisation. We also facilitated the creation of organisational values based on customer research.

Values are the guiding principles that are important and describe actions and behaviours that need to be demonstrated to meet the vision. Values underpin the vision of an organisation and give employees focus on what the business considers to be important.

In gaining internal as well as external customer feedback on the current state of the organisation and the desired state, organisations have the basis from which to formulate or reassess their values.

Working with an organisation in the public sector, I helped facilitate a process of defining values with the governing body and senior management team. The input for this exercise came from internal and external consultation. Once the values were drafted, further consultation took place both inside and outside the organisation to ensure that the values were meaningful and fit for purpose.

Customer service measurement can also be used to measure the application of values both inside the organisation and amongst external customers. (See more on values in Chapter 5.)

Strategy and structure

Often the results achieved by a business have a direct correlation to the vision it aspires to, the values and behaviours it espouses and its strategy, as shown in Figure 8.2. The values and behaviours can be seen as the 'soft' side of a diamond (although often most difficult to influence); strategy is the 'hard' side.

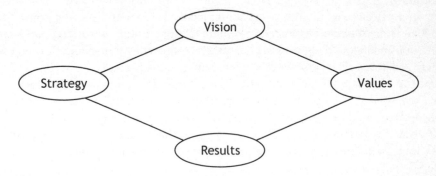

Figure 8.2   Vision, strategy, values, results diamond

Particularly in the public sector, customer consultation and feedback can help drive strategy. In private sector organisations, strategy can be formulated by listening to customers' needs as well as *anticipating* their needs in view of changing market conditions, legislation and other external factors. For example Halifax Bank of Scotland has developed a strategy of e-insurance by funding the organisation e-sure. This is in response to customer's needs for easier, more transparent insurance that can be bought direct over the internet.

Customer feedback can have a direct impact on the structure of an organisation. The structure of an organisation is in turn dictated by its strategy. You need a different structure for an online insurer, for example, than you do for one with branch offices.

When you receive feedback from customers, investigate what structural implications this has. The human resources department in a retail organisation received feedback from its internal customers about the service it provided. The consensus was that human resources were not aligned fully to the business and that it had not sufficient presence in the field. This led to a review of the organisation of the department and its restructuring in line with customers' needs.

Service leadership

Particularly when internal measurement is undertaken that includes attitude surveys, it is probable that improvements are highlighted in the area of service leadership. Indeed many best-practice service organisations encourage their leaders to undertake 360° feedback as part of the performance management cycle.

The leadership style in an organisation shapes the motivation and commitment of employees. Having received feedback, the individual often needs help and support from the organisation to develop leadership skills. This could be in the form of leadership development in-house or externally. Alternatively many businesses now encourage service leaders to engage personal coaches or to find a mentor to support and challenge them.

Competencies and training and development

In Chapter 5, I discussed the use of a competency framework in which customer service is prominent. The results of customer service feedback can inform what skills, knowledge and attitude people need to do their jobs. Customer feedback is a useful starting point, therefore, for the development of competencies. In one travel organisation a working party canvassed customer opinion before designing the business's competency framework. It then consulted customers to validate the competencies for customer facing staff.

Often customer surveys can also highlight areas of training and development needs, be it technical knowledge, such as about a new product or procedure, or interpersonal skills, for example dealing empathetically with complaints. There is a growing trend away from relying on classroom-style training alone. It has been proven that this style of training produces a 24 per cent increase in performance whereas training plus *coaching* produces an 88 per cent increase.

Service standards and service level agreements

Service standards are the operational standards that customers can expect in dealing with an organisation – they specify what the customer can expect and when.

Service standards are useful for:

- focusing team members on the needs of the customer;
- setting expectations with customers and colleagues;
- providing a standard against which you can measure;
- encouraging service improvement.

Feedback from customers provides an ideal opportunity to define service standards based on customer needs.

Typically standards can be defined in areas such as:

- telephone response
- email response
- written response
- visits and meetings
- appearance – of individuals and the environment
- responses to complaints.

To develop service standards it is essential that those people who are instrumental in delivering service see the customer research. They also need collectively to agree standards that are to be put in place. If these are imposed the likelihood is that the standards will not be met. Likewise, service standards should meet the needs of the customer, not the needs of the organisation or the department. Figure 8.3 shows one example of a set of service standards.

Service standards need to be:

- **S**pecific
- **M**easurable
- **A**chievable
- **R**ealistic
- **T**ime-bound

For example, one internal function gained feedback from its customers and discovered that its customers, the unit managers, wanted meetings with the department on a regular

We aim to provide a high quality service to our customers at all times. When you contact us by phone, letter, fax or email, or in person we will:

- Send you a full reply within two working days of receiving your communication.

- If we cannot answer your enquiry ourselves, we will pass your name and contact number to someone who can help within one working day.

- We will answer your telephone calls within three rings.

- We will identify ourselves by name in all communications.

- If you have an appointment with a named person when visiting our offices, they will see you within 5 minutes of the appointment time. If you have not made an appointment, someone will see you within 10 minutes of your arrival.

- If we visit you we will arrive at the appointed time. If there are any unavoidable delays we will call you within 15 minutes of the appointment time to inform of any delay or postponement.

Figure 8.3   Example of one department's service standards

basis. Since meetings at the time took place sporadically, they set a service standard of holding a meeting every three months. The members of the department agreed that this seemed a realistic and achievable time-bound target given that not everyone was currently holding meetings. A year later they were able to improve on this target and hold meetings once every two months, having listened again to their customers.

When setting service standards some people may not believe they can stick to the standard and therefore that this is unrealistic. If this is the case, set a target for how often the standard will be achieved, for example:

We will answer your telephone call within three rings 95 per cent of the time.

You then have a measure to monitor your performance against the next time that you gather customer feedback (see Figure 8.4).

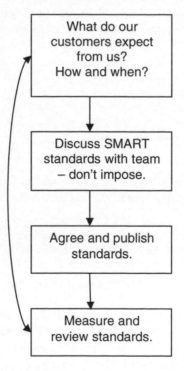

Figure 8.4   The process for setting standards

Both with internal as well as external customers, misunderstandings can revolve around different expectations of the supplier of the service provider and the customer.

Service level agreements are really useful for:

- focusing on what really matters;
- setting and maintaining quality standards;
- pinpointing accountability;
- closing service quality gaps.

IT Department and Training and Development service level agreement

1.   Background and participating parties

The IT department undertakes to provide training and development with a product knowledge intranet-based questionnaire and scoring application. The questionnaire will comprise a maximum of ten sections with 20 questions per section, each section dealing with a particular product.
The sponsors of this agreement are David Hughes in IT and Peter Knowles in Training and Development.

2.   Services to be provided

IT will:

- design templates reflecting Training and Development's corporate 'look and feel' as specified in the published guidelines;
- build a database of product questions together with related correct answers;
- produce a data driven software engine to facilitate question display in random order at each new log in;
- incorporate an email reporting system to monitor user progress;
- integrate the questionnaire with the server;
- work to a two month timescale from delivery of all content to installation; and
- provide helpdesk support to resolve queries and faults from 9.00 a.m. to 5.30 p.m. Monday to Friday, excluding Bank Holidays.

The agreed standard for resolution of queries and faults is 95% resolution within 24 hours from notification.

Training and Development will:

- provide all content including photographs, drawings, graphics, text, logos or any other material to be included in the questionnaire;
- provide and identify the relationship between questions and answers for each section of the questionnaire up to a maximum of 20 questions per section; and
- provide contacts, help and reasonable access to IT personnel and the existing intranet to facilitate the smooth installation of the questionnaire application.

3.   Management of this service level agreement

- Russell Jones from IT will manage this project.

4.   Performance reviews and arbitration

- A review of this service level agreement will take place at monthly intervals after the signing of this agreement.
- If something were to go wrong or become the subject of a dispute Russell Hughes should be contacted first.
- If after discussion a complaint cannot be resolved within two weeks, the two sponsors listed above would aim to provide a mutually acceptable solution within a further two weeks. If the complaint cannot be resolved an independent arbitrator acceptable to both parties would be invited to mediate and their decision would be respected.

Signed   Date:

Training and Development sponsor: IT sponsor:

Figure 8.5   Example of simple service level agreement

Service level agreements are a form of 'contract' between parts of an organisation to control the supply and use of services produced internally or externally. Such services are usually critical to the achievement of objectives.

Those organisations that use service level agreements find that the benefits are:

* greater trust between departments
* improved co-ordination between staff
* improved communication
* greater openness
* acknowledged dependencies
* joint team building
* greater confidence.

There are two types of service level agreement that you can develop:

1 back-to-back – interdepartmental, two way for simple processes
2 complex – multidepartmental, multidirectional for more complex processes.

Figure 8.5 is an example of a simple back-to-back service level agreement. The process for developing a service level agreement is shown in Figure 8.6. A simple service level agreement should contain the following:

1 background
2 participating parties and sponsors
3 services to be provided and for what period

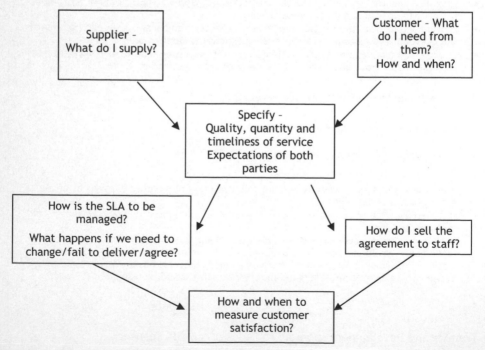

Figure 8.6   Process for developing a service level agreement

4 ordering and delivery procedures
5 agreed performance and service standards
6 responsibilities of the customer
7 performance reviews and arbitration
8 process for changing the service level agreement
9 points of contact for SLA management.

When writing a service level agreement, remember to keep the language simple and unambiguous. The service level agreement should be short; only a few pages, and a maximum of ten. The service level agreement needs to be a 'living' document so mutual exchange of operational information is essential to the effective monitoring of implementation.

Process improvement

In my experience, the results of customer service measurement often highlight the need to improve current processes.

Process improvement is a method for improving the quality, timeliness and accuracy of outputs to customers. It is helpful in:

• identifying blockages and barriers to excellent service;
• improving timeliness and accuracy of output;
• avoiding rework;
• encouraging service improvements;
• encouraging innovation.

A process is a sequence of activities that has inputs and outputs, as shown in Figure 8.7.

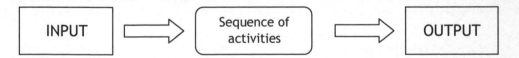

Figure 8.7   A process

There are two types of process improvement that you can undertake:

1 Brown field – making existing processes more efficient and effective;
2 Green field – starting with a blank sheet of paper to completely transform the process.

The steps in the process of brown field improvement are shown in Figure 8.8.

When undertaking process improvement:

• Define each step in the process from start to finish.
• Identify the time taken for each step.
• Identify the people involved.

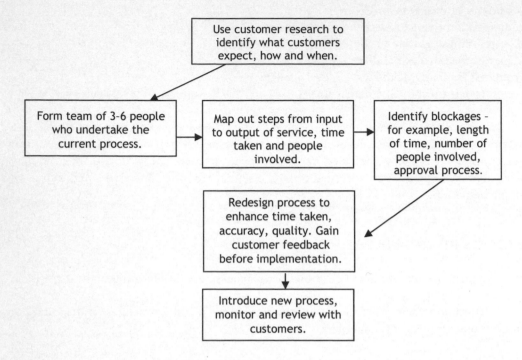

Figure 8.8   Steps in the brown field improvement process

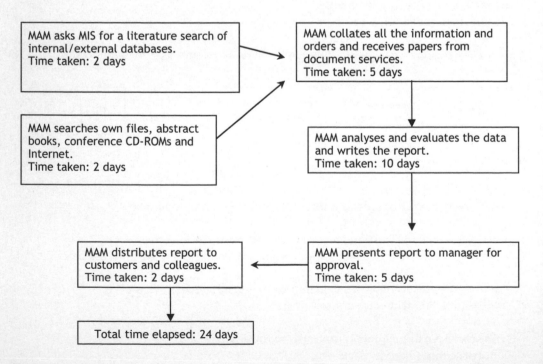

Figure 8.9   Example of existing brown field process for a medical affairs manager (MAM)

- Review the entire process.
- Identify blockages and areas where the process can be shortened.
- Redesign the process so that it takes less time, is more accurate, efficient and results in greater customer satisfaction.

One pharmaceutical company for example wanted to improve the time its medical affairs managers took to produce a report for their internal and external customers. It mapped out the process (see Figure 8.9) and discovered that this lasted 24 days. Through discussions with medical affairs managers, customers and internal suppliers, the project team were able to find ways to reduce this process to 14 days in total (see Figure 8.10).

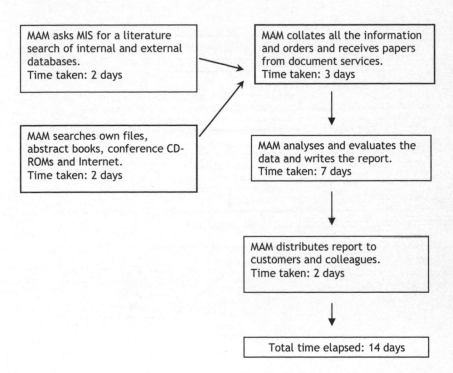

Figure 8.10   Example of improved brown field process for a medical affairs manager (MAM)

If customer research tells you that a new process is needed, it is best to form a team of 3–6 people made up of current service providers and customer representatives. Their task is to start with a blank sheet of paper ignoring the current process and consider:

- What does the customer require?
- What is the best way to deliver this?

Then map out the ideal steps, time and people involved. Next, look at constraints. Challenge these and add them to the process map only if necessary.

The benefits of green field process improvement are:

- encourages re-look at current processes

Dealing with insurance application

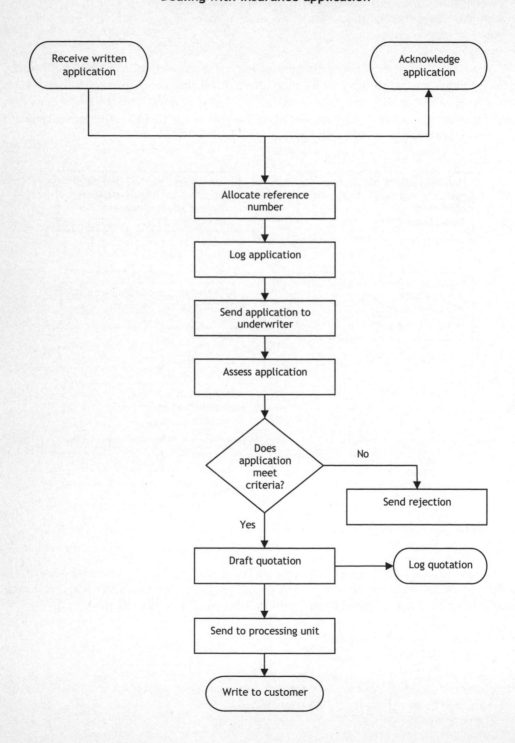

Figure 8.11   Current process

- identifies blockages and time-savers
- encourages team work and co-operation between customer and supplier
- encourages empowerment.

The charts in Figures 8.11 and 8.12 show an existing process for dealing with an insurance application and a green field process. The latter uses web technology to speed the time it takes to process an application and so increases efficiency.

Once you have introduced the new process, monitor it and gain customer feedback.

Dealing with insurance application

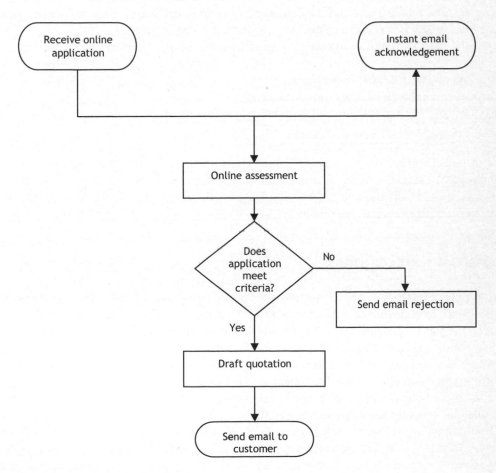

Figure 8.12   Green field process

Service improvement teams

There may be occasions when the service providers do not have solutions to the issues raised by customers. In this instance setting up a service improvement team is a possible way forward for tackling a particular issue or concern.

A service improvement team consists of both customers and service providers who work together to solve service quality issues tantology. Service improvement teams are particularly useful if:

- resolution of a service quality issue needs input from both customers and service providers;
- the service provider needs to gather or pay more attention to customers' views;
- you wish to encourage greater collaboration between the customer and the service provider.

Normally a service improvement team consists of five to eight people, half of whom are service providers (representing all levels – not just managers), and half of whom are customers. The meetings are normally chaired by the sponsor. Many of the problem-solving techniques described in Chapter 7 are useful tools in this sort of meeting.

Having customers in the improvement team benefits the organisation by:

- focusing on the needs of the customer;
- encouraging collaboration and understanding;
- producing joint responsibility and ownership of solutions; and
- ensuring better and more customer-friendly solutions.

Careful consideration needs to be given to when and how to involve customers in an improvement team. If it is not feasible, ensure that there are people who are close to the customer to represent the voice of the customer on the team. This could, for example, be sales people or front line service providers.

Reward and recognition

The outputs of customer service measurement can definitely be used to recognise and reward people who have delivered excellent service. This can be done at an individual level, recognising service providers who have delivered above and beyond the call of duty. It can also be done on a team as well as an organisational level.

Successful companies align reward and recognition schemes to customer service metrics. Harrah's Entertainment in the US linked its customer satisfaction scheme to employee bonuses. It paid out $7 million in the first year of the programme and $12 million in 2001. Its financial performance has surpassed expectations.

By linking pay and reward to customer feedback a business ensures that there is a direct correlation between individual and team performance and the customer. Many companies now have an element of bonus related to customer satisfaction. Yet recognition does not need to be monetary alone. The recognition of a job well done is often worth more to the individual.

One financial services organisation has established an online recognition scheme. This allows managers to nominate staff and peers for acts of excellent customer service. When the person's name is entered, a card can be printed. The manager can also select from a range of rewards that is most appropriate to the individual.

Vision Express fills its head office walls with letters of thanks and praise from its customers. At Claridges Hotel, employees can be recognised by their peers, their managers or a guest. The individual receives a prize from a lucky dip. Prizes range from a stay at the hotel's luxury penthouse suite for a night, through to time off and having a chauffeur-driven limousine drive the individual home.

Remember, introverts probably prefer to be recognised on a one-to-one basis and extroverts on a one-to-many basis. Research has found that the most powerful method of recognition is a 'Thank you and well done' from the line manager in person or in the form of a hand-written thank you note.

Sustaining a customer focus

Customer service measurement is a powerful tool in changing the culture of an organisation, particularly if the results are communicated well and acted on.

Often, there comes a time in any customer service initiative when motivation lapses or customer satisfaction plateaus. The easy part of customer service measurement is establishing a monitoring system. The difficult part is sustaining the measurement system and keeping it relevant and up to date. If the fatigue factor becomes evident in your organisation, it may be time to reassess:

- your sponsor and senior managers' commitment to the current system (it needs to be actively supported and given importance from the top);
- how you undertake the measurement;
- how you analyse and present the results;
- how you communicate the on-going need to improve;
- how you develop improvement plans;
- how you involve others in these plans; and
- the types of improvement you make.

One organisation in the automotive sector had regularly been undertaking customer satisfaction surveys but the enthusiasm for communicating and acting on results had waned. The wake-up call came for them when they added some qualitative techniques to their methodology. Attending and seeing video recordings of the focus groups and hearing customer opinion for themselves shocked the organisation into action. This accompanied by an employee attitude survey meant that the chief executive officer and the senior management team put customer service back on the agenda as their number one priority for change.

OVERCOMING RESISTANCE TO CHANGE

Customer service measurement is a catalyst for culture change. Yet changing the culture of an organisation to become more customer-focused does not happen overnight. Jack Welch, the former chief executive officer of General Electric in the US, reckons it takes at least three to five years.

Studies show that during change people's initial reaction is to ignore what is happening, next comes resistance and the desire to keep the current status quo. Once the change seems inevitable, people begin to explore what this means to them before they become fully committed to the new way of doing things. The problem is that people move through this

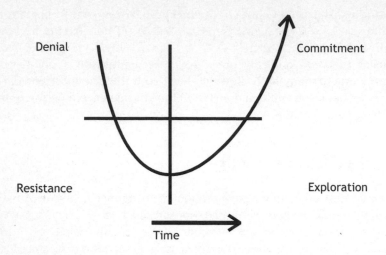

Figure 8.13   Reactions to change

cycle (shown in Figure 8.13) at different paces. In organisations today there is constant change and often the emotional impact of this is not discussed or recognised.

My suggestion is to involve people actively in customer service measurement, to create a group of customer champions throughout the business who can help facilitate a better understanding of customer needs.

Customer champions play a particularly key role during the initial phases of change as they can communicate the need for change and the benefits of this to other employees. They need to be prepared for initial denial of the change – people putting their heads down and continuing on as before. They also need to anticipate resistance to change – people preferring the old way of working. Over time most people begin to test and explore the new before integrating this into their working lives.

CONTINUOUS CUSTOMER SERVICE MEASUREMENT AND ON-GOING COMMUNICATION

Particularly in times of change, people need feedback in order to see how far they have come, celebrate success and raise the bar in terms of performance going forward. I advocate the use of continual customer service measurement so that organisations keep their fingers on the pulse of the customer.

In my experience, it is only when customer feedback is well communicated and employees are involved in actions for improvement that service measurement adds value to a business.

Assess your current approach to acting on results of internal and external customer feedback

Look at the following statements and assess your organisation where applicable:

Customer service measurement criteria	In place	Not applicable	Needs to be acted on or addressed
Our organisation has used internal and external customer feedback to help formulate our vision statement.			
Our company has used internal and external customer feedback to help create our values.			
We listen to customer feedback in formulating our strategy.			
Our organisational structure is dictated by customer needs.			
Our service leaders receive support to develop their leadership skills.			
We have a competency framework and this was developed with reference to customers.			
We provide training and coaching to employees as a result of customer feedback.			

Customer service measurement criteria	In place	Not applicable	Needs to be acted on or addressed
We have set service standards as a result of customer feedback.			
We use service level agreements to manage customer relationships.			
We have undertaken brown and green field process improvement as a result of customer feedback.			
We use service improvement teams made up of customers and employees to tackle specific issues.			
Our reward and recognition scheme is based on customer feedback.			
We regularly review our customer service measurement techniques to avoid the fatigue factor.			
We have customer champions throughout the business who help engender a better understanding of customer needs.			

Customer service measurement criteria	In place	Not applicable	Needs to be acted on or addressed
We measure customer and employee satisfaction and loyalty on an on-going basis.			

Recommended Reading

1001 Ways to Reward Employees
Author: Bob Nelson
UK Publisher: Workman Publishing
ISBN: 156305339X

12 Steps to Success through Service
Authors: Barrie Hopson and Mike Scally
UK Publisher: Management Books
ISBN: 1852523409

A Complaint is a Gift: Using Customer Feedback as a Strategic Tool
Author: Janelle Barlow
UK Publisher: Berrett-Koehler
ISBN: 1881052818

A Passion for Excellence
Authors: Tom Peters and Nancy K Austin
UK Publisher: HarperCollins
ISBN: 0006370624

The Balanced Scorecard: Translating Strategy into Action
Authors: Robert Kaplan and David Norton
Harvard Business School Press
ISBN: 0875846513

Batteries Included! – Creating Legendary Service
Author: Nigel Barlow
UK Publisher: Random House Business Books
ISBN: 0712680632

Best Practices in Customer Service
Author: Ron Zemke
UK Publisher: Amacom
ISBN: 0814470289

Brand Manners: How to Create the Self Confident Organization to Live the Brand
Authors: Hamish Pringle and William Gordon
UK Publisher: John Wiley & Sons
ISBN: 0471496065

Call Centre Savvy: How to Position Your Call Centre for the Business Challenges of the 21st Century
Author: Keith Dawson
UK Publisher: Telecom Books
ISBN: 1578200504

Compendium of Customer Service Questionnaires and Inventories
Author: Sarah Cook
UK Publisher: Gower
ISBN: 0566084287

Customer Care
Author: Sarah Cook
UK Publisher: Kogan Page
ISBN: 0749432365

Customer Relationship Marketing
Authors: Merlin Stone, Neil Woodcock and Liz Machtynger
UK Publisher: Kogan Page
ISBN: 0749427000

Customer Service on the Internet
Author: Jim Sterne
UK Publisher: John Wiley & Sons
ISBN: 0471155063

Customers.com
Author: Patricia B Seybold
UK Publisher: Century/Arrow
ISBN: 0712680713

Delivering Knock Your Socks Off Service
Author: Ron Zemke
UK Publisher: Amacom
ISBN: 0814479707

E-Service: 24 Ways to Keep Your Customers – When the Competition is Just a Click Away
Authors: Ron Zemke and Thomas K Connellan
UK Publisher: Amacom
ISBN: 0814406068

Handbook of Customer Satisfaction Measurement
Author: Nigel Hill
UK Publisher: Gower
ISBN: 0566081946

Loyalty Rules! How Today's Leaders Build Lasting Relationships
Author: Frederick F Reichheld
UK Publisher: Harvard Business School Press
ISBN: 1578512050

The Customer Revolution
Author: Patricia B. Seybold
UK Publisher: Random House Business Books
ISBN: 0712669841

NUTS! Southwest Airlines' Crazy Recipe for Business and Personal Success
Authors: Kevin and Jacquelyn Freiberg
UK Publisher: Orion Business
ISBN: 075281334X

Once a Customer, Always a Customer
Author: Chris Daffy
UK Publisher: Oak Tree Press
ISBN: 186076164X

Practical Benchmarking
Author: Sarah Cook
UK Publisher: Kogan Page
ISBN: 0749422270

The Service Profit Chain
Authors: James Heskett, Earl Sasser and Leonard Schlesinger
Simon & Schuster, Inc
ISBN 0684832569

Twenty Training Workshops for Customer Service
Author: Sarah Cook
UK Publisher: Gower
ISBN: 0874251931

Index

About Sarah Cook and The Stairway Consultancy

Sarah Cook is the Managing Director of The Stairway Consultancy Ltd. She has 15 years' consulting experience specialising in service excellence and culture change. Prior to this Sarah worked as a marketing manager for Unilever and as head of customer care for a retail marketing consultancy.

Sarah has practical experience of helping public and private sector organisations measure their service effectiveness. She is passionate about excellent service. Most of Sarah's work is based on the principles of the service profit chain: effective leadership leads to high levels of employee satisfaction, which in turn generates customer satisfaction, retention and profit. Sarah has written widely on the topic of service excellence. She also speaks regularly at conferences and seminars on the topic.

Sarah heads The Stairway Consultancy. Stairway is a management consultancy dedicated to helping organisations increase their focus on the customer. In this way they successfully enhance their clients' ability to retain customers and maximise their long-term profitability. The Stairway philosophy is holistic. We believe that the investment in a strategy of service excellence is a long-term one and its philosophy needs to be endorsed from the top. Measuring service effectiveness is a key method for bringing the voice of the customer into the heart of the business.

Stairway's services include:

- Helping organisations develop vision and values and a service excellence strategy.
- Facilitating both quantitative and qualitative measurement of external and internal service including one to one interviews, questionnaires, employee surveys and facilitation of external and internal customer focus groups.
- Using customer feedback to help service providers develop service standards and service level agreements.
- Development of competency-based frameworks linked to service excellence.
- Training in how to run a customer focus group.
- Experiential and skills-based training for service leaders.
- Development of recognition schemes linked to service excellence.
- Training of internal facilitators to help bring about change.
- Consultancy in all aspects of service excellence and culture change.

Stairway's style of working is under-pinned by our core values:

Customer-focus: we place high value on adding value to our clients, on meeting their needs and delivering excellence service.

Partnering: we place high importance on building close, long term relationships that are both supportive and challenging. We work collaboratively to find a way forward rather than to impose our own solutions.

Learning: we place high value in continuing to learn and develop and encourage others to do the same.

Integrity: we keep our promises, are open, honest and fair.

Passion: we work in areas and use approaches that we have energy for and are passionate about; we encourage others to do the same.

Diversity: we work with a diversity of consultants, clients and approaches in order to increase the opportunities for creativity. We work from the basis that people generally want to be and do their best.

For more information about The Stairway Consultancy please see www.thestairway.co.uk or contact sarah@thestairway.co.uk.